Letters to
A College Student:

On the Light of Reason and the Search for Truth

Robert Stackpole

Chartwell
Press

PUBLISHED BY
THE CHARTWELL PRESS
www.thechartwellpress.com

Robert A. Stackpole, STD
Director of the John Paul II Institute of Divine Mercy
Assistant Director of Formation,
St. Therese Institute of Faith and Mission

ISBN: 978-1514227671

Printed in the United States of America
July, 2015

8/28/16

Dear Saoirse,

Hope you enjoy reading this
as you start your college career.

Love,
Grammy (Gramma)

For Christina:
To help light the way

Table of Contents

Foreword

It is all too possible in studying the part to lose sight of the whole. If one stands very close to a painting one may learn certain things about the paint that was used, but may not be able to say anything about what the painting depicts. It would be a tragedy to learn all that could be learned about the nature of the paint but never experience the painting. A very real danger in the great good of attending university is that one learns in the various disciplines how to study the 'paint' in great detail, but gets little instruction on how to see the 'picture'. Indeed, in a postmodern climate suspicious of any sort of metanarrative, one may be informed by one's professor that, genuine insight into objective reality is impossible, such a picture is impossible, and that pursuit of it inevitably leads to the oppression of those with whom one disagrees.

Yet we do yearn to find unity and meaning in the diversity of experience; a unity and meaning that we do not impose on reality, which can be brought to light by reflecting on experience. In his *Letters to a College Student: On the Light of Reason and the Search for Truth*, Robert Stackpole makes the case that reason, combined with honest investigation, reveals a world that witnesses beyond the possibility of reasonable doubt to the truth of Belief in God. His marshaling of evidence in a cumulative case argument is impressive.

Robert A. Larmer, PhD
Professor and Chair, Philosophy Department,
University of New Brunswick
Author, **Dialogues on Miracle**.

i

1. Can We Really Know Anything for Sure?

Dear Krystal,

Thank you so much for your wonderful letter—what a delight to hear from you, my favorite niece (OK, my *only* niece—but still my favorite)! I know very well that the transition from living at home to life in a university dorm can be a huge one, but from what you have written, it sounds as if you are experiencing far more than just a change in lifestyle: your thinking and your faith are evidently being challenged as never before. It's not necessarily a bad thing: real wisdom has to pass through a refiner's fire before it can become strong enough to do us much good. Your letter shows that you are already being "singed" a bit by the intellectual heat!

I was especially intrigued by one paragraph from your letter, which I will quote back to you here, and then share some thoughts with you about it. You wrote:

> It seems that nothing is certain to anyone here at this university, or at least there is no consensus about what to believe. Everyone has a different point of view. For example, one of my profs is a practicing Buddhist. He says that everything that we perceive to be so "real" and troubling is just an illusion; until we learn to "see through" such illusions, we will never be able to chill-out and find inner peace. My French professor, on the other hand, is a passionate lover of the novelist Albert Camus. He told us the other day that until we honestly come to terms with our own death, as Camus did, we can never really grow up and become "authentic" individuals (cheerful stuff—especially since his class meets at 8 in the morning when I usually feel half-dead anyway!). Some of the students here don't seem to believe in much of anything at all except their weekend parties and getting drunk on a regular basis—or worse. I made a few friends at the

student Environmentalist Club, but they mostly seem to be atheists. They were talking the other day about the latest books they had read by the "New Atheists" such as Hawking and Dawkins, and how the natural sciences such as physics and chemistry are the only things that can be trusted to give us hard facts, the "objective" truth about the world. Anything else, they said, is sheer fantasy or wishful thinking. Of course, I largely kept my mouth shut, not wanting to seem a "dinosaur" to them on first meeting because I think I still believe there's a God…. I wonder what to think these days. Almost all of these people I meet are very intelligent and sincere, yet they disagree with each other on what to believe. Sometimes I think that in this crazy, "post-modern" world, the only prudent thing to be is an "agnostic," a doubter: I mean, just admit that no one can really be sure of anything anymore.

Well, Krystal, you know that I write about these "big questions" for a living (in other words, I get paid for sharing what I think about such things, which is a blessing!). So I doubt you will be surprised if I take the liberty of commenting a bit on your thoughts here, especially your retreat into the safety of "agnosticism." The agnostic claims not to be sure about anything, and as you said, in our so-called "post-modern" world, where there is so much disagreement surrounding even the most basic truths about the universe and the meaning of life, agnosticism may seem a safe, humble, and tolerant stance to take.

There is only one problem: I don't think anyone can really take it.

You see, you may claim to be unsure about everything— for example, about the existence of God, about right and wrong, about life after death—but at every minute of the day, from the time you get up in the morning until the time you fall asleep at night, you are living as if *something* was true; you must believe in something strongly enough to base your daily life upon it. For example, the fact that you bother to get up in the morning at all implies that you believe that there is something good or beautiful that is worth getting up in the morning and seeking for, at least for one more day. The fact that you feed and clothe yourself implies that you believe pretty strongly that you exist, that you have a body, and that taking some kind of minimal care of it may help you move forward in your search. The fact that you may never stop to pray during the day shows that however "agnostic" you may claim to be about the existence of God, you are actually living each day as if He did not exist—or, to be more precise, treating Him each day as if He did not exist. The fact that you open the news page on the internet and recoil with horror when you see the mangled bodies of the victims of another terrorist attack implies that you know for sure that some things at least are "objectively" morally wrong—I mean, that no one ought to do such things, ever—such as blowing up innocent children on a school bus. If need be, you would support and cooperate with the law enforcement authorities in any reasonable efforts they take to put a stop to such crimes.

The point is, you can't really take the "agnostic" option in any of these areas of life: either you get up in the morning with hope or you don't; either you feed and clothe yourself because it's worthwhile doing so or you don't; either you spend some time relating to God in prayer each day or you don't, you either live out a commitment to basic moral values or you don't. Life goes on. You cannot "sit on the fence" of any big question that affects your daily life—and most of the big questions do—just because you cannot sit on the fence of life. You have to live each day as if something was true, whether you want to or not, and the way you live, on a regular basis anyway, betrays what you really believe.

You haven't taken a Philosophy course yet, Krystal, but when you do you will find that the guy who most famously wrestled with this question—"Can I know anything for sure?"—was the 17th century French Philosopher Rene

Descartes. He reasoned like this: It seems at first that I can doubt everything. After all, everything I experience could be nothing more than an illusion or a dream. Still, even if that was the case, there would be one thing I could know for sure: my own existence. For if I am suffering from an illusion, there must be someone here being deceived, and if everything I experience is a dream, there must be someone here doing the dreaming. In other words, I can try to doubt everything, but at least there must be someone here doing the doubting. So Descartes came up with what he believed was the one, rock-bottom certainty, the first, foundational thing we can all be sure of: one's own existence, as a thinking self. "I think, therefore I am," he wrote. And on this rock-bottom truth he tried to build his whole philosophy.

No doubt Descartes was right that we can be certain of our own existence, and it would be self-contradictory to say otherwise—but what he failed to see was that there were many other things he was also sure about at the same time, or he never could have come up with his insight, "I think, therefore I am," in the first place. In fact, there are a whole bunch of common sense and self-evident things we can know with confidence, and each one of them is bound up with the others—none of them can stand alone.

For example, just to assert "I think, therefore I am," is to rely upon the validity of the most basic principle of logic, called "The Law of Non-Contradiction." This rule states: "a thing cannot both be true and not be true, in one and the same sense, at one and the same time." Sounds difficult, but really it's as simple as a child's game of peek-a-boo. When you play peek-a-boo with an infant, what is the baby laughing at? He or she is laughing because Mommy's face can either be visible, or not visible—but not both at the same time. In other words, the child is laughing in wonder at the discovery of the most basic fact about reality: direct contraries cannot exist, and be true, at one and the same moment. Every child knows this—Descartes forgot that he had assumed it to be valid all along. For to say "I think, therefore I am," is at the same time to say "It would be false to say I am not." To know and assert anything as true is to know that it's direct opposite is false.

Without realizing it, Descartes also assumed the truth of the general meaningfulness of human language: that the words he was using made sense. To argue as he does that we can attempt to doubt everything because everything we experience might be an illusion or a dream implies that those words "illusion" and "dream" have some real, discernible meaning. Think about it: how would we know what the word "dreaming" means except by contrast with experiences we have had of another state in which were not dreaming at all, but "awake"? And how would we know what the word "illusion" means except by contrast with experiences we have had where we knew for sure that we were not being deceived at all? Thus, if we were dreaming everything we experience or deceived about everything we experience, we could not even know the meaning of the words "dream" and "illusion" to begin with!

The plot thickens now because we can only really know the meaning of certain crucial words Descartes used, such as "illusion" and "dream," if we are thinking selves with real physical bodies. After all, how could we ever know what "illusion" means unless we had, at least once in our lives, "unmasked" an illusion with the help of our five bodily senses? In other words, we know what an "illusion" is because at least once in our lives we have double-checked, by further sensory investigation, what merely *appeared* to be true at first. For example, you may have discovered that stainless steel spoons do not really bend in a simple glass of water—although they appear at first to be bent in the water—because you reached your hand in the water and found, with your bodily sense of touch, that the spoon was still straight. In this way, you "unmasked" a visual illusion, and confirmed what an "illusion" is—but you had to rely on the help of your five senses to do it. Again, I can only know what "dreaming" is by

5

contrast with the state of "wakefulness,"—but what is wakefulness other than the state in which our sensory experiences are supremely vivid and intense? That's why we commonly say, "pinch me and make sure I'm awake"! You can dream a lot of things, but you cannot dream the real feeling of a bodily pinch. So, Descartes thought that we can be sure of our own existence as thinking subjects apart from any sure knowledge that we have physical bodies, but in this he was surely mistaken.

We could go on, Krystal. There are many other things that you and I are sure about—and Descartes was too, although he didn't realize it. Many philosophers believe that language is essentially a social creation, designed for communication between thinking selves. We seem to have a natural capacity for it, but that capacity in us cannot develop and be put to use apart from interaction with other people. You may have heard of the famous case of Eccles, a 13 and ½ year old girl who had been found isolated from birth from all human contact. She had no "private" language at all, and could only begin to form the most simple words and sentences after several years of human interaction. In short, the mere fact that Descartes was using human words at all to think and to write out his thoughts implied that he had already interacted with other people, and that with them he had learned to use a common language to express his thoughts and communicate.

Do you see what I am driving at? Descartes thought that the first and foundational thing we could be sure about was our own existence as thinking subjects, but in fact, we can only be sure about that if we also know with confidence, at the same time, that we are bodily and social beings, and that basic standards of logic apply to all our statements, and that the words we use have real meaning.

And we could go further. One could argue that there are also basic, self-evident truths of mathematics and morals that everyone knows for sure are true, but that no one can strictly "prove." They are simply among the network of common sense beliefs that we all live by every day, and never seriously doubt for a moment—and (here is the most important thing) *no one has ever come up with any strong reasons for doubting them.* Again, Descartes assumed the truth of a whole bunch of these things without even realizing it. And so does every so-called "agnostic" who gets out of bed in the morning and goes about his business.

Philosophers sometimes call these things "self-evident propositions" or "properly basic beliefs." How do we know for sure what these properly basic, indubitable beliefs really are? The 18th century Scottish philosopher Thomas Reid gave us some very simple tests for spotting them:

1) They are universally held (in other words, no one genuinely doubts them, except those whose mental equipment has been impaired by illness, alcohol, or drugs);

2) We are irresistibly drawn to them from childhood;

3) They are indispensable to everyday living.—and, I would add, they can sometimes be corroborated in everyday living. (This one is fun, Krystal, because you can tease sophisticated agnostics at your university with it. They live by these "properly basic beliefs" every day, even while claiming to be in doubt. For example, next time you go with one to the pub, order a round of drinks for everyone, and then insist that your agnostic friend pay for them. Watch him squirm and grumble about the unfairness of it all—but if we cannot be sure about anything, that must include the properly basic moral standard of "fairness"!)

It is possible that something people once thought of as a properly basic belief—for example, that the sun really travels across the sky—might be shown to be fallacious; but the burden of proof lies on the doubters here. Without overwhelming evidence to the contrary, we are surely justified in holding these properly basic beliefs as "true beyond a reasonable doubt."

A helpful thing to do with your doubting friends is to ask them if they have any reasons for their skepticism. As soon as they offer you some, you can easily show that their "reasons" for being skeptics actually assume in advance the truth of many "properly basic beliefs." For example, a friend might say that he is generally skeptical of our ability to know the truth about the world because peoples and cultures often disagree about such things. But that assumes that other people exist, that we can communicate with them through meaningful language, and that the Law of Non-Contradiction applies to any meaningful discourse (after all, how could peoples and cultures fundamentally "disagree" with each other if their viewpoints were not contradictory?). In other words, once someone offers any reasons at all for their point of view, those reasons already assume the truth of something— including a bunch of "properly basic beliefs." And if, by contrast, someone cannot or will not give any reasons for their point of view, why should we bother to take their perspective seriously?

Of course, philosophers disagree with each other about how "properly basic beliefs" come to reside in our heads in the first place. Some say that our intellect can come up with them simply by reflecting on our sensory experience of the world. Some say our brains must be "hard-wired" by evolution to believe certain things because they help us survive as a species. Some say that at least some of these properly basic beliefs (especially the common standards of "perfection" we have in our minds such as "perfect justice" or a "perfect circle") must have a "transcendent" source, in other words, a source outside of us; perhaps these standards are beamed into our minds by God, who is Infinite Perfection Himself! I tend to think that the truth lies in a combination of all three of these ways.

Anyway, Krystal, I certainly won't drag you into that debate now! Suffice it to say: you already know a lot more things for sure than you may realize—and so did Descartes—and the great thing is that, just by standing on these properly basic beliefs, these common sense realities, you can reach as high as the heavens.

So, when someone at college tells you that the safe and humble thing to do these days is to be a complete agnostic, a doubter, because "you can't be sure of anything at all," just say in reply: "I wouldn't be so sure about that!"

Love,

Uncle Robert

2. The Problem with "Nothing Buttery"

Dear Krystal,

OK: I know it was not fair to end my last letter by promising you that there was some easy way to "reach for the heavens"—and then saying nothing more about it. And I know I failed to say anything at all about your scientific-atheist friends. I understand from your letters that your university campus is full of "buzz" these days about the so-called "New Atheism," so I guess I might have said something about all that. Since you are inviting me to do so now, I will certainly try.

As I understand it, the New Atheists claim that the only thing we can really be sure about is what can be proven by the scientific method of observation and experiment. In other words, only the natural sciences can give us the facts, the real "objective truth." Anything else—religion, judgments of moral value and beauty—are just "subjective opinions" or comforting sentiments at best, or superstition and bigotry at worst.

What scientists can now tell us, the New Atheists say, is that they are on the verge of coming up with a scientific "Theory of Everything": a law or set of laws that can fully explain the origin and evolution of the universe and everything in it, without any need for belief in God. This means that literally everything could be explained in terms of atoms and molecules, and the mathematical laws that govern their behavior. Human life itself, on this reckoning, is only the chance product of the natural laws that govern the evolution of life on planet earth ("survival of the fittest"). So any ultimate meaning or purpose for human life can only be found by examining our place in the story of evolution, and the development and survival of life on this planet. The only objectively "right" way for human beings to live, therefore, is the way that best promotes survival of our species, and of the whole evolutionary biosphere that gave birth to us.

In short, in the New Atheism we have what astrophysicist Rodney Holder of the Faraday Institute in Great Britain has called the theory of "Nothing Buttery." This is the theory that the whole universe, and everyone and everything in it, is "nothing but" matter and energy, atoms and molecules (or more precisely, quarks and gluons) bouncing around in space according to mathematical laws. Imagine the universe as like one gigantic popcorn popping machine, with all of the kernels bouncing around inside it for billions of years, and you get a fair idea of what they mean.

What the New Atheists don't seem to acknowledge is that fundamentally there is little that is "new" about "Nothing Buttery." The ancient Greeks had their own version of it in the philosophy of Democritus. Also known as "Reductionism," it has been kicking around again since the 18th century, summed up by the famous scientist Laplace:

> We may regard the present state of the Universe as the effect of its past and the cause of its future. An intellect which at any given moment knew all the forces that animate nature and the mutual positions of the beings that compose it, if this intellect were vast enough to submit its data to analysis, could condense into a single formula the vast movement of the greatest bodies of the universe and that of the lightest atom: for such an intellect nothing could be uncertain; and the future just like the past would be present before its eyes.[1]

OK, so what's the problem with Nothing Buttery?

To begin with, while many of the New Atheists are accomplished scientists, very few are accomplished students of Philosophy. It's all very well to claim that the only thing we can be sure of is what can be verified by the scientific method: the trouble is, *you cannot prove that claim to be true by the scientific method.* Try devising a scientific experiment to prove that only the natural sciences can give us objective truth! It's simply not possible. What some of the New Atheists are asking us to accept, therefore, is just their own blind faith in the natural sciences as the *only* path, the *only* method for finding the objective truth about this world in which we live.

I am not knocking the natural sciences, Krystal: of course, they tell us lots of important and useful things about the physical world. Because of the natural sciences, we know more than ever before about the age, expanse and early history of the cosmos, the appearance of living things on earth and their interdependence in "ecosystems" on our planet. As a result, we can be more responsible stewards of our natural environment, making sure that we do not pollute and destroy what God and nature have passed down to us. Moreover, we can now enjoy all the blessings for human life provided for us by modern science, such as information technology (the internet, etc.), modern medicine, travel, and agriculture. Clearly, the natural sciences have vastly increased our capacity for wonder at the awesome design of the universe in which we live, and have rolled back a fair amount of human misery in the process.

Still, there are many important things that we know for sure that do not come from the natural sciences. Think of all the "properly basic beliefs" I listed in my last letter. Why would anyone even bother to engage in scientific investigation in the first place if they did not already know for sure that they exist, that they have human bodies that inhabit a natural world that really exists, and that they can investigate this world with their five senses, and make true statements about its order and structure which can be understood in meaningful language and mathematical terms by other human beings? Scientists must believe and presuppose all of this before they even get started!

Beyond all that, scientific investigation cannot make progress unless scientists themselves are entirely committed to some properly basic moral beliefs, for example, the principle of truth-telling: that scientists should honestly report (and not invent) their own findings.

Moreover, the whole scientific enterprise is based on a key presupposition—another properly basic belief: that reality is consistent, that the small slice of the natural world we observe through our microscopes and telescopes is an accurate microcosm of the entire natural world. In other words, scientists have to believe—and cannot strictly prove—that the order of nature and the laws that describe it persist in *all* parts of the universe, at *all* times: past, present and future. These laws are not true today and gone tomorrow, or true in Texas but not in the Andromeda galaxy. The validity of the same laws of nature in all parts of the universe at all times is indeed a remarkable feature of the universe. As Albert Einstein famously remarked, "The most incomprehensible thing about the universe is that it is comprehensible."

Most the great early scientists were Christians (for example, Copernicus, Kepler, Galileo, Descartes, Pascal, and Newton). They were actually propelled into the scientific study of the world by their faith: their belief that all of nature must have a uniform rational order because it is the creation of a single, all-powerful and rational God. Atheists who are scientists have to believe in the uniformity of nature too, but in their case it's simply an act of faith. Summing up the perspective of many others, astrophysicist Rodney Holder has written:

> Scientists in going about their business exercise a kind of faith. They rely on the order and rationality of the world. And it is very hard to see where this order and rationality, and the applicability of the same laws across all of space and time, could come from except there be a single source for them, namely God.[2]

My point is, Krystal, that there are lots of things scientists have to believe that the natural sciences cannot prove, or science could not progress at all.

Besides, there are realities that human beings experience every day that cannot be reduced merely to atoms and molecules bouncing around in space. "Nothing Buttery" just cannot offer a complete explanation of it all. For example, what is love? Have you ever experienced the love of another person (I know you have Krystal, because I know your family well!)? Can your experiences of love simply be reduced to a series of chemical reactions in your brain? No doubt chemical reactions in the brain are involved every time you experience anything at all, but how can someone prove that such physical events are all that is going on, say, when your mother takes care of you, or your friend sits down with you and listens to you share your problems over a cup of coffee? How about the beauty of poetry or symphonic music? Can these too be reduced merely to chemical responses and reactions in the brain? And how about the universal human desire to find meaning and purpose in life?

Some rather bold evolutionary scientists do indeed claim that we can explain all of these aspects of human life on the basis of their "survival value." Maybe these things—love and friendship, poetry and music, meaning and purpose—just calm our nervous systems enough to enable us to survive as a species! But consider: how could good poetry and music really bring us much comfort, and help make life worth living, unless we sincerely believed they opened us up to a realm of beauty and value that goes beyond our mere need for biological survival? And what biological survival-benefit could there be in the agonizing search for the meaning of life, which leads many people, after all, only to suicide or despair? And what biological survival-value could there be in commitment to moral values that involve the proper care and respect for the dignity of *each and every human being*—even the weak, the broken, those "unfit" for survival? Every code of human rights that humanity has ever written proclaims loud and clear that human dignity is not based merely on survival value! Surely we ought to treat each other with dignity and respect, no matter whether it lengthens the life span of our species or not.

In fact, we now know that even in the natural, physical world we simply cannot explain everything in terms of the mathematical behavior of atoms and molecules. For example, there are complex systems in the natural universe which cannot be fully understood or explained on the basis of the laws of physics that apply to its parts. Scientists call these "emergent" properties. The physical "wetness" of water, for example, has no meaning at the level of a few water molecules, but requires an aggregation of many water molecules. "Wetness" is an emergent property of water that is neither predictable nor fully comprehensible on the basis of its molecular structure alone.

"Emergent" properties of nature are even more evident in living creatures. For example, a simple living cell has "information transfer" going on within it all the time, as the DNA within the cell "communicates" with other parts of the cell to enable the cell to grow and develop. But "information transfer" cannot be deduced from, nor fully understood in terms of the physical and chemical structure of DNA alone. Even the concept of "information" itself is meaningless apart from the function and purpose of the cell as a whole, in other words, there is evidently what philosophers call a level of "teleology" going on in the biosphere: cells and parts of cells seek to function to achieve purposes. To deny all this would be a bit like trying to understand what a "book" is simply by analyzing the chemicals and physical laws involved in the paper and ink that the book is made out of: you would totally miss out on the information, the message, that the book was conveying!

The claim that scientists may soon find a mathematical Theory of Everything is also doomed to failure because of modern advances in mathematics. Now you know very well that I am no mathematician, Krystal. It's a good month if I can just succeed in balancing my bank account, much less attempting more difficult equations! But I do know that the 20th century witnessed a revolution in the field of mathematics which makes the search for a mathematically based explanation for Everything an impossible quest. Physics is based on mathematics, but we now know that mathematical systems themselves can never be completely explained or proven. Rodney Holder sums it up like this:

> What is very surprising is that, in any system at least as complex as arithmetic, there exist statements which we know to be true, yet which cannot be proved. To put it another way, you cannot have a consistent mathematical system which is also complete. This remarkable fact was discovered by the eminent Austrian mathematician Kurt Godel and is known as Godel's theorem.[3]

What this means is that if we try to explain everything in terms of physics, and physics itself in terms of mathematical laws, we will run into a dead-end of explanation, because mathematics cannot fully explain or prove itself!

Once again, Krystal, it's clear that there are many aspects of our human experience, and even of the physical universe, that "Nothing Buttery," or "Reductionism," can never account for. Everything in the universe simply cannot be "reduced to" atoms and molecules.

Finally, one of the biggest problems of Reductionism is that it can only really answer the "how" questions we ask (how does the natural universe of matter and energy behave?) but it cannot even begin to answer the "why" questions. For example, why is there something rather than nothing at all? Why is there a high degree of order in the universe rather than sheer chaos? If we are genetically programmed merely for biological survival, why do human beings seek for meaning and purpose, and a life of fulfillment even beyond death? As

Steve Jones, Professor of Genetics at University College, London put it in the Reith Lecture series of 1991:

> It is the essence of all scientific theories that they cannot resolve everything. Science cannot answer the questions that philosophers—or children—ask: why are we here, what is the point of being alive, how ought we to behave? Genetics has almost nothing to say about what makes us more than just machines driven by biology, about what makes us human. These questions may be interesting, but scientists are no more qualified to comment on them than is anyone else.[4]

Perhaps the best answer of all to Nothing Buttery is simply the famous quote from Shakespeare's *Hamlet*: "There are more things in heaven and earth, Horatio, than are dreamt of in your philosophy."

Arguably the greatest scientist of the 20th century, Albert Einstein, had this to say about the harmony possible between science and religious belief. For the true person of science:

> His religious feeling takes the form of a rapturous amazement at the harmony of natural law, which reveals an intelligence of such superiority that, compared with it, all the systematic thinking and acting of human beings is an utterly insignificant reflection. This feeling is the guiding principle of his life and work, in so far as he succeeds in keeping himself from the shackles of selfish desire. It is beyond question closely akin to that which has possessed the religious geniuses of all ages.[5]

And here is another great quote from Einstein, Krystal, which you can share with your New Atheist friends whenever they tell you that science alone can give us "objective truth," and that science will soon be able to explain Everything: "Science without religion is lame; religion without science is blind."

With Love,

Uncle Robert

3. The Human Spirit

Dear Krystal,

Well, you got "clobbered," and I am sure you are right: it was largely my fault. I encouraged you to try that quote from Einstein that I gave to you on your atheist friends, and the "pounding" you got in response was something I should have prepared you for—or at least warned you about. I really did not mean to send you off "like a lamb to the slaughter"—I'm so sorry!

If I've got it right, what they said to you in a nutshell, in front of everybody in the pub, was something like this:

> Organized religion has been responsible for more ignorance and superstition, bigotry and intolerance, wars and persecutions than anything else in all of human history. No self-respecting educated person should have anything to do with it.

Quite a slap-down!

When things cool off a bit you might try to gently clarify the truth about these matters for your friends. For what they said is simply not true. As a matter of fact, the proverbial "shoe" is largely "on the other foot": it is *organized atheism* that has been responsible for more persecution and death than any other social movement in history. In the 20th century alone, atheist regimes and ideological movements bumped off more innocent people through wars they started and human rights abuse than all the religious wars and persecutions from all centuries put together! Just be fair and do the math: Hitler, Lenin, Stalin, Mao, Pol Pot, Castro, atheist totalitarian regimes in Cuba, North Korea, China, Southeast Asia, Russia and throughout Eastern Europe. These all led to the Soviet "purges" and gulags, the Maoist "re-education" camps, the "killing fields" of Cambodia, revolutionary violence and communist attacks on Korea, Vietnam and Afghanistan, the deliberate starvation of the Ukraine, Nazi attempts at genocide and world domination—the list goes on and on. The net result was the direct killing for political and ideological reasons of at least 80 million people. (Some would drop Hitler and the Nazis from this list because Hitler manipulated the religious sentiments of his people to get elected, and many of his closest followers were bizarre pantheist-occultists and not real atheists; to my mind, however, Hitler was the ultimate atheist, because he actually worshipped *himself* as God. In any case, even without Hitler and the Nazis, the single century death-toll is still at least 60 million).

It's not clear that the victims of all the wars and persecutions driven by primarily religious motives down through history add up to even 20 million. The main crimes here would include those medieval Crusades that were truly needless, the Spanish Inquisition, a few attempted Muslim invasions of Europe (at Tours, Lepanto, and Vienna), the extent to which British and American slavery were falsely justified by religious arguments (although it was devout Christians who led the abolition movements too), the 16-17th century European witch hunts, the Protestant-Catholic 30-years war, the massacre of Armenian Christians by the Turks, and the Sunni-Shia armed conflicts. All of this was grim behavior indeed by people who claimed to believe in a God of mercy and compassion. But again, *it was spread over 20 centuries*, and numerically "small potatoes" compared with the horrors that atheist regimes accomplished in just one.

Add to that the body-count from *disorganized atheism*: since the Soviet Communists first legalized abortion early in the 20th century, several hundred million innocent unborn children have been put to death in their mother's wombs around the world—mostly by unbelievers. In short, if we are really serious about massive abuse of human rights, and understanding what causes it, then we need to "call a spade a spade"; from the French Revolution's Reign of Terror onward, atheism and anti-religious ideology has been by far the bigger culprit.

In a recent book entitled ***Field of Blood***, noted historian of religion Karen Armstrong has met head-on the claim that religion is a major cause of social violence. The charge is simply not backed up by the historical facts. A review of her book in the New York Sunday Times (December 24, 2014) sums up her research like this:

> First, through most of human history, people have chosen to intertwine religion with all their other activities, including, notably, how they are governed. This was "not because ambitious churchmen had 'mixed up' two essentially distinct activities," she says, "but because people wanted to endow everything they did with significance."

> Second, this involvement with politics means that religions have often been tied up with violence: Crusaders, conquistadors, jihadists, and many more. But—a point Armstrong cares about so much that she makes it dozens of times—the violence almost always originates with the state and spills over to religion, rather than vice-versa….

> [For example], "As an inspiration for terrorism…nationalism has been far more productive than religion." And religions face the dilemma of whether to accept the protection of the state, and the threat of violence that this necessarily entails, or to live in hermetic isolation….

> In nearly all cases, she argues, violent impulses that originated elsewhere—with nationalism, struggles for territory, resentment at loss of power—may have presented themselves as "religious" disputes but really had little to do with faith…. An overemphasis on religion's damage can blind people to the nonholy terrors that their states inflict.

Attacking religion in general for being the source of violence and persecution is a bit like attacking sex because it has resulted in so much rape, incest, child abuse, adultery, family breakdown, and sexually transmitted disease down through history. The fact is that *anything* important to human life and flourishing can be (and has been) grievously misused over the centuries (the same could be said of love of country, and love of nature). The solution is not to do away with religion, sex, patriotism and love of nature: the solution is to foster wholesome versions of these things. Besides, given the social track record of the alternative (the track record of organized and disorganized atheism, outlined above), as well as the social decay all around us today in our fully secularized society— with its record levels of divorce, abortion, suicide, substance abuse and violent crime—and I am pretty sure that a religion-free world is not the answer!

Anyway, Krystal, Christians who start wars of aggression or brutally persecute religious minorities can only do so by ignoring or distorting the fundamental tenets of their faith: "God is love;" "Love your neighbor as yourself;" "Love your enemies;" "all people are made in the 'image of God,'" etc. It's like swimming up-stream. But when you think about it, there is little in atheist ideology that justifies belief in the dignity of each and every person. Atheist regimes and social movements are founded on the principle that the individual is of little value apart from his or her "usefulness" to the economy, to the nation, to the "will of the people," to the survival of the species, to the ideal socialist state or to the master race. It does not take a rocket-scientist to figure out that where human life is held to be only of worldly, "instrumental" value, then at some point many of those human "instruments" will get labeled as socially useless or unfit—and then thrown on the rubbish heap. In addition to that, leaders of atheist regimes seldom have to worry that they will ever be held accountable for their crimes against human dignity. After all, according to them there is no God and no Judgment Day—so ultimately no one is answerable to anyone for anything.

I know that your agnostic friends, Krystal, would have a response to all this. They would say: "You see, that's what happens when anyone, whether they believe in God or not, thinks they know for sure what the meaning of life is: they inevitably try to impose their beliefs on everyone else."

That attitude is understandable, Krystal, but I think it misses the heart of the problem. As far as I can see, the driving force behind persecution and intolerance has not been that people believe something too strongly: rather, it has been the *content* of what people believe in so strongly. If you believe passionately that human life is only good for this world, and useful for nothing more than the support of some social or political program, then the persecution of those who do not support or cannot usefully build up that program is sure to follow. But if you honestly and passionately believe that we are created by a heavenly Father who made each of one us in His image and loves each one of us infinitely, how can you possibly (without violating your core beliefs) persecute and murder your brothers and sisters? Yes, some people have done just that—it's tragic—but it's self-contradictory. No one can coerce anyone else into an authentic state of faith and love. Rather, the most logical thing for the committed believer in God to do is to seek to share the truth he believes he has found with those who have not found it yet, through personal witness and evangelism: in other words, to propose rather than try to *impose*. A fair look at the historical record shows that by and large, that is what Christian missionaries—albeit imperfectly—tried to do.

Meanwhile, it was believers in God who first established constitutional protections for fundamental human rights. In the Declaration of Independence of 1776, the Founding Fathers of the United States based human rights on the Creator's design: "We hold these truths to be self-evident, that all men are created equal, that they are endowed by their

Creator with certain unalienable rights, that among these are Life, Liberty, and the pursuit of Happiness." These rights were held to be "unalienable"—that is, irrevocable by human governments and social institutions—because of their divine source: they come from God and not from humanity or society. Thomas Paine, Patrick Henry, Thomas Jefferson, John Adams, James Madison, Alexander Hamilton, John Jay, George Washington—all without exception strongly believed in the existence of an all-powerful, all-wise and benevolent God as the best foundation for liberty and democracy.

By contrast, the Reductionist, Nothing Buttery view of human nature almost inevitably undermines respect for human rights. Pope John Paul II, who lived through both the Nazi and the Communist occupations of Eastern Europe in his lifetime, summed up the matter like this;

> The root of modern totalitarianism is to be found in the denial of the transcendent dignity of the human person who, as the visible image of the invisible God, is therefore by his very nature the subject of rights which no one may violate— no individual, group, class, nation, or state. Not even the majority of a social body may violate those rights by going against the minority, by isolating, oppressing or ignoring it or by attempting to annihilate it.[1]

Generally, Krystal, people treat other people either as "things" (mere objects, whether useful or useless) or as real "persons." If you believe that human beings are just objects, nothing but a collection of atoms and molecules (Nothing Buttery again!), merely animals with more advanced brains, doomed to be swallowed up by death in the end, then that is probably going to have a dramatic effect on how you relate to other people, and even to yourself.

The perspective of classical Philosophy, however, is that there is a deep mystery about each one of us. We are not just animal bodies made up of matter and energy bouncing around in space. There is a depth and personal dignity to each one of us: the human "spirit," a well-spring of longing for truth, beauty, and goodness. In Philosophy we sometimes call this deepest aspect of ourselves the "soul." To be more precise; the human "soul" is a "spirit": in other words, unlike physical objects, it is not located in space, and it does not have separable "parts." It can cause things to happen in and through its human body, but it also can do remarkable things that no bodily or physical machine could ever do: it can reason, it can love, and it can long for the infinite, that is, for truth, beauty, and goodness that transcends time and space.

The human spirit can do these amazing things best in conjunction with its body, but it is not a bodily entity. This also means that it cannot decompose like a bodily thing. Physical objects composed of parts can decompose and fall-apart, but not the human spirit. As F.J. Sheed once wrote:

> Material beings can be destroyed in the sense that they can be broken up into their constituent parts; what has parts can be taken apart. But a partless being is beyond all this. Nothing can be taken from it, because there is nothing in it but its whole self….
>
> A spiritual being, therefore, cannot lose its identity. It can experience changes in its relation to other beings—e.g., it can gain new knowledge or lose knowledge that it has; it can transfer its love from this object to that; it can develop its power over matter; its own body can cease to respond to its animating power and death follows for the body—but with all these changes it remains itself, conscious of itself, permanent.[2]

In classical and Christian philosophy, as you know, Krystal, God Himself is an infinite "Spirit." He is not a bodily creature. Since He is confined to nowhere He can be present everywhere, and do all that "Spirit" can do—reason and love—to an infinite and boundless degree. The human spirit is just a little reflection, a little image, of that Infinite Spirit.

How do we know that we have this deep mystery inside each and every one of us?

The 13th century Philosopher St. Thomas Aquinas can help us here. In his writings he argued that the human soul is the immaterial and immortal aspect of the human person.

Saint Thomas offered several philosophical arguments for this belief. In the human mind and heart, he said, we find many activities which, considered in themselves, transcend the power of matter. For example, unlike any other living creature, the human mind can conceive and know more than purely material things, such as "love," "justice" and "God," and this shows that the human mind is not itself material. For example, we should not be able to work out an abstract theory of physical science were the human mind nothing but atoms and molecules (again, abstract concepts are not material things). Furthermore, self-consciousness is a sign of the immaterial character of the human mind: as human beings we can not only think, we can be aware of ourselves thinking and reflect on ourselves thinking—an incredible mystery! And the same can be said of free choice. If our choices were always just physical events in our brains, and nothing more, then they would be involuntary reactions to other physical events happening in our brains, and not "voluntary" actions at all.

If St. Thomas had lived in the 21st rather than the 13th century, he would have at his disposal further indications, drawn from the natural and social sciences, to bolster his claim that human beings each possess an immaterial, immortal soul. For example, psychologists have noted that Siamese twins and identical twins, although possessing the same genetic make-up, and in most cases virtually the same formative environment, can end up with dramatically different personalities. This implies that there is a third element at work, beyond our genes and environment, which makes us the kind of persons we are. That extra element is the human spirit. In addition, there are all those documented cases of people who have been pronounced dead, medically speaking, and yet who mysteriously came back to life again. They commonly describe their experiences as "out-of-the-body" and "life after life" experiences. If you can be "out" of your body, then there must be some aspect of you that is not your body. That aspect is your soul.

Then there is the evidence for free-choice complied by Canadian neurosurgeon Wilder Penfield. He experimented on willing human subjects who were undergoing brain surgery under local anesthesia, and were therefore fully conscious (the brain has no pain receptors, so it didn't hurt!). He found that electrical stimulation of the motor cortex of the brain, the part of the brain responsible for movement of the limbs, gave rise to actions disowned by the patients. In other words, the patients described the actions of their limbs, caused by such brain stimulation, as actions done to them, not by them. There is clearly something different about the way our motor actions are processed when they are done voluntarily (that is, when they proceed from our free choice), as opposed to when they are just caused by electrical activity in the brain. This suggests that our acts of free choice arise first of all from our immaterial soul, and not from our brain alone.

Furthermore, scientists have now discovered that our brains are not immutably wired from birth or infancy. Physician Jeffrey Schwartz has shown that brain systems can to some extent be re-wired by positive or negative mental activity. This has long been common sense any way: who does not know that a positive mental attitude can help reduce blood pressure, or that people can get well merely by believing that they are being given the right medicine to take, even if that medicine is actually only a "placebo"? Clearly, there is something about our conscious selves that goes beyond mere brain-states, and that can even alter and re-wire our physical brain capacity.

It is important to recognize that for St. Thomas Aquinas, the relationship between the human body and the human soul is a very close one. Body and soul are certainly distinct aspects of the human person, but they are literally "made for each other." Some people get confused about this. As soon as they come to believe that we each possess an immaterial, immortal soul, they start to think that the "soul" is the real "me," and that the human body is unimportant.

On the contrary, according to St. Thomas the human body and the human soul need each other. On the one hand, the body needs the soul to be the body of a living human person. In fact, when the soul definitively separates from the body, that is what we call "death." On the other hand, the soul needs the body too. In order to gain most kinds of knowledge, the soul needs the sensory data and visual images provided by the body in order to have something to think about. Most forms of knowledge come from the soul reflecting upon, and drawing conclusions about, the data provided by the five senses of the body.

Think about it: if you want to form a relationship with me, how do you do it? In most cases, the only way is by speaking words with your lips, or making signs with your body, or using your fingers to type out sentences on a computer. All of these physical things (sound waves, visual images) are then picked up by my body and stored in my brain, and then my soul can reflect upon them: "Wow! This person is eager to communicate with me—eager to be my friend, or to tell me to get lost!" Without our bodies, interpersonal communication and human relationships would be nearly impossible. So would all of the arts and sciences. How could your immaterial soul play a piece of music on a piano or perform an experiment in a medical laboratory without a body? The soul has these potentials for attaining knowledge, for creative self-expression, and for interpersonal relationships, but without the assistance of the body we could never fulfill these potentials, they could never come to fruition. That is why St.

Thomas once wrote: "It is not to the detriment of the soul that it is united to a body, but for the perfection of its nature."

That is also why, as a good Christian theologian as well as a philosopher, St. Thomas welcomed the biblical doctrine of the final "resurrection of the body"; because a human being is not just a soul without a body (that's a poltergeist), nor a body without a soul (that's a zombie or a corpse), but a compound of body and soul, to the perfection of both aspects of human nature. Our final destiny is not merely to be everlasting, disembodied spirits, like Casper the Friendly Ghost! Rather, Christians believe we are to be raised on the last day in the fullness of our humanity, in a glorified body and soul, in the same way that Jesus of Nazareth, our Savior, was raised on Easter morning.

Peace to you in Him, Krystal. I will try to write again when I can; there is so much more to say about the mystery of you and me, the great mystery of what it means to be human!

Love,

Uncle Robert

4. The Difference It Makes

Hi Krystal,

Great to hear that your midterm exams went so well—and of course, I am delighted that your study of French and World Literature is really igniting your interest. I hope to see you at Christmas, when you can help me practice my French too. Sadly, I have forgotten most of it over the past few years.

I was not surprised at all by what you wrote to me in response to my last letter: that you have never really considered the mystery of the human "spirit" before. Of course you haven't, because no one ever taught you about it! How many high school programs these days really bother to introduce young people to the Great Thinkers of Western Civilization: Socrates, Plato, Aristotle, Augustine, Aquinas, Dante and Shakespeare, for example? Our education system is cutting students off from the wisdom of the past, as if these folks had nothing of lasting importance to teach us. They may not have much to teach us about the natural sciences, but they have plenty to teach us about what it means to be fully "human"!

Sorry; that's just me "grinding an axe" of mine again.

I promised you that when I found a bit of time I would write more about these matters. As you know, I am now convalescing at home after minor surgery, so that gives me plenty of time to kill: time enough, certainly, to carry on our dialogue.

I am heartened that you take such a keen interest in these questions, Krystal, and that you are such a sincere and honest seeker of the truth. I guess you are discovering along the way that you do not have to be a professional philosopher or a brainy intellectual to be able to ask, and find some answers to many of life's biggest questions (Can I know anything for sure? Is the universe "nothing but" atoms and molecules? Is the scientific method the only way to find "objective" truth? What is a human being? Do human beings have souls as well as bodies?). You don't need a philosophy degree to tackle these questions: just a clear head and an honest heart.

Going back to my last letter for a moment, according to the philosopher St. Thomas Aquinas, a human being is an *embodied spirit*: a bodily creature with an immaterial soul that has the capacity for rational thought and free choice, and a longing for infinite good.

This makes us unique in the universe, as far as we know, and in any case creatures with an extraordinary potential for creativity, wisdom and love. Moreover, given that the human spirit is immaterial, that is, not composed of parts, it cannot decompose; it is naturally immortal. In all these ways, according to Aquinas, the human spirit is a living reflection of the Infinite, Divine Spirit.

Oh, I know what some people would say to all this. They would say that the whole idea of immortality—of life after death or "pie in the sky when you die"—was just cooked up by the ancient and medieval ruling classes, and their priests, to convince slaves and other laborers to "keep their noses to the grindstone," so to speak, forget about justice or happiness in this life, and put all their hope in the life to come.

The historical facts, however, do not bear out such conspiracy theories. In his book, *Life After Death: The Evidence*, Dinesh D'Souza summed up the historical testimony on this matter:

> One of the most striking things about the afterlife is that belief in it is absolutely universal. This point is clearly established in Alan Segal's magisterial study *Life After Death*. Segal shows that every culture, from the dawn of mankind, has espoused some concept of continued existence....Segal recognizes, of course, that not every individual in those cultures expected to have life after death. In fact, most early cultures made provision only for the future life of the ruling

aristocracy. The peasants and ordinary people were not considered important enough to warrant consideration for the afterlife….

These facts refute the idea that ancient religion was merely a tool for elites to reconcile the common people to their lot by promising them a wonderful existence in the next life. In reality, ancient cultures only attended to the postmortem prospects of their pharaohs and rulers.[1]

Marxist scholar Eugene Genovese, in his famous study of American slavery entitled *Roll, Jordan, Roll*, discovered that even the slave system of the old American South was not really based upon teaching slaves to resign themselves to their fate through by offering them promises of heavenly reward. D'Souza again explains:

Genovese began his study expecting to find that Christianity reconciled slaves to their condition by telling them to wait for their eternal salvation and not to expect freedom in this life. This is precisely what atheists allege. And Genovese did find that the hope of eternal vindication did sustain many of the slaves during the dark night of their captivity. But Genovese was amazed to discover that such heavenly expectations never taught the slaves to become reconciled or contented with their lot. Rather, the slaves developed a powerful ethos of liberation, one in which the hope of salvation in the next world was inextricably connected with the demand for freedom in this world. Genovese, who later converted to Catholicism, shows how the slaves read the Bible to develop this ethos. Consider the lines of the great spiritual "Go down, Moses, way down to Egypt land and tell old Pharaoh, let my people go." Here from the book of Exodus, the slaves drew an analogy between their own condition and that of the Israelites under Egyptian captivity. In this way Moses became a champion not only of the Jews in captivity, but also of the African slaves in America, and many freed slaves later named their children "Moses." Contrary to the atheist critique, the Bible provided the slaves a great message of liberation.[2]

Anyway, it stands to reason, doesn't it, Krystal? If you honestly believe that human life is of such value and dignity that in some sense it can continue and flourish forever, then that is all the more reason to believe in the dignity of human life in this world as well, and to uphold and protect that dignity on the road to heaven.

In short, we cannot side-step the philosophical and scientific case for the immortality of the human spirit on the basis of half-baked historical conspiracy theories. To consult Philosophy and Science about what it means to be a "human being" is just common sense—since every one of us is one! I remain convinced that reason can show that we are creatures with tremendous personal dignity, and an eternal destiny.

And it seems to me that this classical, philosophical view of the human person—which is also shared by Christianity and Judaism—helps us avoid the pitfalls of two pernicious errors about human life that have plagued mankind from the beginning of human history.

First, there is the view that the "real person" or "essence" of a human being is something completely spiritual. Thus, for some of the ancient Greek philosophers such as Plato and Plotinus, the human soul was seen as "imprisoned" in the human body, as if temporarily trapped in a tomb. At best, the body was seen as something that the immortal soul can use for a time and then discard at death, kind of like a snake shedding a skin it does not need anymore. Plato said that the human soul is present in its body like a sailor is present in his ship: he uses the ship for a time to get where he needs to go, and then happily jumps out when he reaches his final destination.

In general, the body with its passions and lusts was considered by the Greeks a distraction from life's highest goal: the philosophical contemplation of truth. For some eastern religious traditions, the individual human body, like all passing and transient things, is even seen as unreal, an illusion (didn't you tell me, Krystal, that one of your professors more or less believes this?). We see an echo of this belief in the "Christian Science" movement: the view that all bodily sickness is illusory. The advanced practitioner of Christian Science allegedly has no need of medicines. He or she just needs to use his advanced faith to see through the illusion of illness, and it will no longer plague him!

The philosophers of the 17th and 18th century Enlightenment, such as Leibniz and Kant, believed that human beings have both immortal souls and material bodies, but they could not give a clear and convincing account of the connection between the two. Body and soul seem to have no clear interrelationship, since on their view the presence of the body makes very little difference to the soul, and the soul makes very little difference to the body.

Anyway, if you buy into one of these viewpoints, Krystal, that the human soul is the only thing about us that really exists or that really matters, then it can have a profound effect on how you live your life. For example, you might end up as a drop-out mystic, who tries to forget his bodily self as much as possible in order to promote purely spiritual states of contemplation; or maybe you will end up as an old fashioned Puritan who sees the human body as nothing more than a constant source of temptation (and therefore you might completely shun such bodily things as drinking alcohol, dancing, and the creative arts). Or you might end up as an intellectual snob who believes that only the higher, intellectual life is worth living, and that only lower forms of human beings engage in manual work; or you might end up as the kind of missionary who believes that only "saving souls" is important, and neglects making an effort to heal the sick, feed the hungry, and speak out against social injustice. Or you might end up as the kind of person who believes that only your "spiritual" relationship with the divine is important, and so it does not matter what you do with the rest of your life as long as you keep up your religious practices—a greedy, money-grubbing, materialistic lifestyle is nothing to worry about.

In short, there are many false pathways down which the hyper-spiritual person may wander.

Most people today, however, are far more likely to take the opposite path: the path of those who sincerely believe that human beings have no immaterial "soul" at all. Such people believe that what we traditionally call the "powers" of the soul, such as rational intellect and free choice, are really just physical reactions, chemical and electrical events in our brains. In reality, we are nothing more than "naked apes" (as a popular book from the 1970s put it). After all, isn't that what modern science tells us? We know, for example, that physical disturbances can produce mental disorders, and that some mental disorders can even be cured by medical treatment. Thus, a blow on the head can cause amnesia, or a person can take pills to alleviate depression and schizophrenia. Neurology shows us that something happens in our brains every time we think a thought or feel an emotion or make a choice. So doesn't that prove that *everything* we used to think of as going on in our "souls" is really just the result of electro-chemical reactions going on in our heads? For people who think this way, Krystal, human beings are "nothing but" animals equipped by evolution with more advanced cranial computers.

Nothing Buttery, however, simply doesn't work. Just to drive the point home, I'll expand upon the philosophical arguments and scientific evidence for the human spirit that I offered last time.

First of all, do you remember in my last letter how I mentioned the scientific evidence for out-of-the-body, life-after-life experiences? In his famous 1975 study of this subject, physician Raymond Moody reported on 150 cases of people from a wide range of backgrounds who had gone through near-death experiences, and he found that in many cases these experiences were virtually identical. D'Souza again sums up the evidence for us:

> In this…composite account, a person shows the clinical signs of death or is pronounced dead by his doctor. Yet far from losing all awareness, he hears a loud noise and finds himself moving swiftly through a dark tunnel. He is now outside his physical body and can see it from a distance. (This is the out-of-body experience my wife had following her accident.)… He encounters the spirits of relatives and friends who died. In some cases he reports seeing Jesus or other celestial beings. He is also dazzled by a bright light that envelops him with warmth and love. The subject now finds his whole life before him, so that he can panoramically review or evaluate it.[3]

Moody's research was subsequently confirmed, and extended—so much so that there is now an International Institute for Near Death Studies. Moreover, further research has shown that not all experiences of life-after-life are positive ones; in a substantial minority of cases the soul encounters dark and fearful realities too.

A clever refutation of these phenomena was offered by scientist and philosopher Carl Sagan in his book *Broca's Brain*. Sagan suggested that at our life's end and under duress, we return in memory to the original birth process. Thus, common reports of floating through a dark tunnel of light are not really evidence of a journey to immortality: they are just a distant memory of our original journey down the birth canal.

Sagan's skepticism, however, does not stand up under scrutiny. Research on infant perception shows that newborns cannot see anything as they proceed down the birth canal and emerge from the womb. Moreover, infants hardly float down a tunnel of light as they are being delivered: rather, they are squeezed, sometimes suffocated and often bruised by the whole ordeal. It is hard to see how a distant memory of *this* experience forms the basis for the out-of-the-body, life-after-life experiences reported by so many near-death survivors.

Here is a second argument, Krystal, for the existence of the human spirit: abstract rational thought cannot be completely reducible to physical states of the brain. While any computer can process numerical equations, abstract thought involves using and comprehending universal concepts such as "truth,' "goodness," "beauty,"—even "nature" and "human being." There simply cannot be a one-to-one correspondence between abstract concepts and brain states. For example, physicist Rodney Holder asks us to consider the many physical forms that "money" can take, from paper bills of all colors and sizes, to silver coins, Spanish dubloons and digits on a stock trader's chart. And yet this variety of visual stimuli on the eyes, producing very different physiological effects on the brain, is somehow all interpreted as the same abstract, universal concept: "money."

Third, ask yourself this question, Krystal: how much do abstract thoughts and universal concepts weigh? How long are they? How tall are they? In the same vein: what is a free choice made out of? Can you package it and sell it in a drug-store? And is conscious self-awareness a solid, liquid, or a gas—or maybe a certain high voltage electrical current? In other words, isn't it intuitively obvious that acts of abstract rational thought, free choice, and self-conscious awareness are not reducible to physical states that can be measured and quantified?

Fourth, if all our thoughts are just the result of electro-chemical reactions going on in our brains, and nothing more, what reason would we have to trust them? Many philosophers have argued that there is an inherent self-contradiction in this strictly "materialist" view of the human mind. Why should you and I trust our own minds if they are nothing but thinking machines, programmed by chance, by the random processes of nature? Would you trust a computer that had been programmed by a bunch of monkeys randomly banging away on a computer keyboard?

Of course, our minds might be programmed by evolution to think practical thoughts that enable us to find food, shelter, sex, and survive, but how would the process of evolution give us any grounds for trusting in our capacity for more advanced, abstract thought—including the validity of such abstract notions as "Evolution" and "Nature?"

To bring it closer to home: why should I trust my own thoughts at all if they are merely the product of the random assortment of chemicals and electrical currents flowing through my brain cells on any given day? If what I believe today is solely the product of how I was brought up, the health of my nervous system, and what I had for breakfast this morning, why should anyone, including me, take any of my beliefs seriously? But notice carefully where this takes us, Krystal: for if my mental processes are solely determined by the chance collision of atoms in my brain, and I have no reason to trust them, then I also have no reason for supposing that my mind is composed of nothing but the chance collision of atoms in my brain. In short, if human rational thought is "nothing but" the random interaction of atoms and molecules, then I have no reason to trust in human rational thought—which means I have no reason to trust any arguments on offer that the human mind is "nothing but" atoms and molecules. In this case, Nothing Buttery saws off the branch it is sitting on!

Fifth, if I do not have an immaterial soul or spirit that can make free choices—that is, if my will, my choosing-power, is wholly determined by physical causes—then I am really nothing but a robot, completely "pre-programmed" by my genes and my environment to think whatever I think and do whatever I do. How then can I be held to be responsible for my actions? How can I be asked and expected to live up to some code of moral behavior? Moral codes tell us how we "ought" to behave, but that implies that we "can" behave in accordance with moral principles if we so choose. If we have no real free choice, then what becomes of this idea of "ought," and personal moral "responsibility"? Rodney Holder sums up the matter like this:

> If we are nothing but atoms and molecules organized in a particular way through chance processes of evolution, then love, beauty, good and evil, free will, reason itself —indeed, all that makes us human and raises us above the rest of the created order—lose their meaning. Why should I love my neighbor, or go out of my way to help him? Rather, why should I not get everything I can for myself, trampling upon whoever gets in my way?... The best we can do would be to come to some kind of agreement in our mutual interest…to live in peace, but if it suits us we shall be free to break any such agreement. Our behavior could degenerate to what we see in the animal world—after all, we are just animals anyway.[4]

So, Krystal, if you hold the Reductionist view of what a human being is, it can have a dramatic effect on how you live your life. For example, you might end up as a sensualist or hedonist, that is, as someone who lives primarily for bodily comfort and pleasure. Many gluttons, lechers, and drunkards fall into this category, as well as the multitudes trapped in the shallow, materialistic "consumer" culture in which we live (have you noticed that the center of most cities today is no longer the cathedral, or even the town hall, but the shopping mall?). Or you might end up convincing yourself that human life is driven primarily by economic forces. "All history is the history of class struggle," the Marxists claimed, and therefore they devoted themselves to the revolutionary struggle of the working class, and to the dictatorship of the workers party, the Communist party. Or you might hold that human beings are indeed primarily economic animals, but that economics is really about "survival of the fittest": so the realistic thing to do is to get rich any way you can, no matter who you have to cheat and exploit to do so. Or you might hold with the Fascists that the fundamental fact about the human animal is his genetic inheritance, and that some races are evidently genetically superior to other races, and therefore the best thing for the world would be for the master race to take charge and rule (or exterminate) all inferior races.

Finally, like many who have lost their belief in the created dignity and eternal destiny of the incredible body-soul creatures that we are, you might just one day sink into despair, believing that death swallows all. Playing "the Devil's advocate," Christian Philosopher William Lane Craig summed it up like this:

> Mankind is a doomed race in a dying universe. Because the human race will eventually cease to exist, it makes no ultimate difference whether it ever did exist. Mankind is thus no more significant than a swarm of mosquitoes or a barnyard of pigs, for their end is all the same. The same blind cosmic process that coughed them up in the first place will eventually swallow them all again.[5]

As Shakespeare's Macbeth put it, on this reckoning human life is ultimately nothing more than "a tale told by an idiot, full of sound and fury, signifying nothing."

You see: understanding the mystery of who we are, Krystal, really does make a difference. The value and dignity of human life depends on it!

Love,

Uncle Robert

5. The Secret
of the Human Heart

Dear Krystal,

Something tremendous has happened to you. That's clear from your letter.

I cannot say I know a lot about the Norse Mythology you have been reading in World Literature, but I do at least remember the Germanic stories of *The Ring of the Nibelungen,* because I remember my Dad taking me to see the great operas by Wagner based upon them when I was a boy. Mysterious and magical tales indeed!

I understand that when you watched portions of those operas with your class, the stories became more than just another great set of fantasy tales. For you they became what the Irish call "a thin place": a place where the veil between worlds, suddenly, unexpectedly, became translucent. I mean, for you they became the occasion of something truly awesome: an experience of the *mysterium tremendum.*

I know you may not be familiar with that phrase; it comes from the academic study of religious experience. But you wrote about it without realizing it:

> I just wanted with all my heart to be within that magic Circle of Fire when it surrounded the sleeping heroine Brunhilde; I just wanted to follow the Norse gods when they journeyed up and up into Valhalla; I wanted to cry out: "Please take me with you! Please don't leave me behind! I don't want to stay here; I want to be with you!" A ridiculous desire, I suppose, but that's how I really felt. Like how I felt at times when my Dad read to me the *Chronicles of Narnia* when I was little. Narnia is where I belong; it's my true home. So what am I doing here? And how can I find the door in the wardrobe again that will take me there?

It's not ridiculous at all, Krystal. I have felt it too. I think everyone has at one time or another, if they were willing to admit it. The Romantic poets and composers of the 19th century knew all about it. We like to laugh today at the excesses of "Romanticism"—but I am convinced they were on to something.

I remember when I was a teenager going on a summer camping trip with friends. We hiked into the deep woods for several miles until we came upon a shelter, a "lean-to," at the base of a forested hill, with the open side facing a broad fresh-water stream. The water flowed down the hillside, winding as it went, cascading over the rocks at every turn. As that stream water splashed and swirled, it almost sang to us, and when twilight came, I felt this desperate, inconsolable longing to follow that stream up the hill, right to its hidden source—at the same time knowing full well I could never find it. And all the while, the stream sang its mystery to me, and comforted me in my grief.

I can never forget that evening. It was only years later that I heard a piece of music by the composer Ravel (I think it was the start of his Daphnis and Chloe, suite #2) that in some distant way captured what I had experienced of that stream in the twilight.

It has happened to me other times as well. I remember it was Christmastime, and I was staying at my parents' home in New York. I woke up one morning, and gazing at the bedroom window, saw that there was fresh snow falling. In my drowsy state I looked out of that window upon a birdbath in the back-garden below. Everything in the garden was blanketed with snow: the azalea bushes, the dogwood trees, even that little birdbath was gilded with white, as several sparrows and finches perched upon it and rinsed their feathers in the not-quite-frozen water. It was a vision of perfect peace and tranquility, perfect beauty. For a few brief moments, everything was just as it ought to be, and I drank it in like a man dying of thirst, longing for it not to change, and knowing very well that it would.

It's funny that you should mention *The Chronicles of Narnia*, Krystal, because their author, C.S. Lewis, wrote more about these kinds of experiences than anyone else I know. In fact, it was one of the reasons that he and his friend J.R.R. Tolkien wrote their fantasy stories in the first place: to try to unlock this secret that we all keep buried within ourselves, this painful desire that we try to smother with food and drink, sex and pleasure, radio and t.v., burying ourselves in an avalanche of consumer goods and "busy-ness" in order to deaden the pain. But Lewis and Tolkein would not let their readers forget their longing for home. Lewis once wrote in his essay, *The Weight of Glory*:

> We want... something the books on aesthetics take little notice of. But the poets and mythologies know all about. We do not want merely to see beauty, though, God knows, even that is bounty enough. We want something else which can hardly be put into words—to be united with the beauty we see, to pass into it, to receive it into ourselves, to bathe in it, to become part of it. That is why we have peopled air and earth and water with gods and goddesses, nymphs and elves—that though we cannot, yet these projections can enjoy in themselves that beauty of which Nature is the image… Do you think I am trying to weave a spell? Perhaps I am; but remember your fairy tales. Spells are used for breaking enchantments as well as for inducing them. And you and I have need of the strongest spell that can be found to wake us from the evil enchantment of worldliness which has been laid upon us for nearly a hundred years.[1]

I am going to quote for you here several long passages from Lewis's writings on this subject, Krystal, just because they are some of the most important words he ever wrote—and to save you the trouble of looking up the passages yourself (I know you have more than enough to do to get ready for your end-of-semester exams!).

First, in a famous passage from his autobiography *Surprised by Joy*, Lewis describes for us these experiences of painful longing:

> I will only underline the quality common to [these] experiences; it is that of *an unsatisfied desire which is itself more desirable than any other satisfaction.* I call it Joy, which is here a technical term and must be sharply distinguished from both Happiness and from Pleasure. Joy (in my sense) has indeed one characteristic, and one only, in common with them; the fact that anyone who has experienced it will want it again. Apart from that, and considered only in its quality, it might almost equally well be called a particular kind of unhappiness or grief. But then it is a kind we want. I doubt whether anyone who has tasted it would ever, if both were in his power, exchange it for all the pleasures in the world. But then Joy is never in our power and pleasure often is.[2]

Notice what he says at the end of this passage: that "Joy is never in our power." That's really the same thing you said in your letter to me: you said that no matter how many times you went back and listened to those operas of the Ring story, even to the very moments in those operas that had so deeply moved you, you could not seem to re-create the same feelings. All you had left was the sweet memory of those experiences, not the experiences themselves. So, whatever you had been longing for, it was evidently not just the endless repetition of opera highlights—otherwise the return to the highlights would have been an encore experience of "Joy" as well.

It's the same for me. I went back to that stream in the forest in later years—several times—but while those visits brought back the memory of that sweet, inconsolable desire, I was never able to re-create the experience itself. It's just not in our power to do so.

And even if we could go back and recreate those desires, it would never satisfy us. After all, it was not the waterfall itself, or the winter snow that I really wanted—it was something else, something that those beautiful objects and moments only hinted at, like hearing the strain of distant music.

Lewis described other aspects of "Joy" in the third edition of his book *The Pilgrim's Regress*, which fit perfectly with your experience, and mine:

> The experience is one of intense longing. It is distinguished from other longings by two things. In the first place, though the sense of want is acute, and even painful, yet the mere wanting is felt to be somehow a delight. Other desires are felt as pleasures only if satisfaction is expected in the near future: hunger is pleasant only while we know (or believe) that we are soon going to eat. But this desire, even when there is no hope of possible satisfaction, continues to be prized, and even to be preferred to anything else in the world....

> In the second place, there is a peculiar mystery about the object of this Desire. Inexperienced people (and inattention leaves some inexperienced all their lives) suppose, when they feel it, that they know what they are desiring. Thus, if it comes to a child while he is looking at a far off hillside he at once thinks, "if only I was there;" if it comes when he is remembering some event in the past, he thinks, "if only I could go back to those days." If it comes (a little later) while he is reading a "romantic" tale or poem of "perilous seas and faerie lands forlorn," he thinks he is wishing that such places really existed and that he could reach them. If it comes (later still) in a context with erotic suggestions he believes he is desiring the perfect beloved. If he falls upon some literature...which treats of spirits and the like with some show of serious belief, he may think he is hankering for real magic and occultism. When it darts out upon him from his studies in history or science, he may confuse it with the intellectual craving for knowledge.

But every one of these impressions is wrong…. For I myself have been deluded by every one of these false answers in turn, and have contemplated each of them earnestly enough to discover the cheat.[3]

This may be the deepest mystery of all about you and me, Krystal, and indeed about the entire human race. We are told that we are creatures genetically well suited by evolution to match our natural environment in this world—then why do we so painfully long for something that nothing in this world can satisfy? What possible biological "survival value" could these repeated, inconsolable experiences of "Joy" have for our species, except to keep us searching for the unattainable, and in a perpetual state of grief for never having found it?

"Nothing Buttery" has no resources to explain this, only pathetic attempts to explain it away. But even the proponents of Reductionism admit, when their guard is down, that this is the painful secret of their own hearts too. The leading 20th century atheist philosopher Bertrand Russell, for example, wrote this in his autobiography: "The center of me is always and eternally a terrible pain—a curious wild pain—a searching for something beyond what the world contains, something transfigured and infinite."[4]

Well, bless old Bertrand Russell for his honesty. What he was willing to admit in passing, however, Lewis treated as the central mystery of his own life story. In his book, *Mere Christianity*, Lewis shared with his readers the conclusions he had come to about his lifelong search to unveil this mystery:

Most people, if they had really learned to look into their own hearts, would know that they do want, and want acutely, something that cannot be had in this world. There are all sorts of things in this world that offer to give it to you, but they never quite keep their promise. The longings which arise in us when we first fall in love, or first think of some foreign country, or first take up some subject that excites us, are longings that no marriage, no travel, and no learning, can really satisfy. I am not now speaking of what would ordinarily be called unsuccessful marriages, or holidays, or learned careers. I am speaking of the best possible ones. There was something we grasped at, in that first moment of longing, which just fades away in reality. I think everyone knows what I mean. The wife may be a good wife, and the hotels and scenery may have been excellent, and chemistry may be a very interesting job: but something has evaded us.

Now there are two wrong ways of dealing with this fact, and one right one.

(1) The Fool's Way—He puts the blame on things themselves. He goes on all his life thinking that if only he tried another woman, or went for a more expensive holiday, or whatever it is, then, this time, he really would catch the mysterious something we are all after. Most of the bored, discontented rich people in the world are of this type. They spend their whole lives trotting from woman to woman (through the divorce courts), from continent to continent, from hobby to hobby, always thinking that the latest is 'The Real Thing' at last, and always disappointed.

(2) The Way of the Disillusioned, 'Sensible Man'—He soon decides that the whole thing was moonshine. 'Of course,' he says, 'one feels like that when one's young. But by the time you get to my age you've given up chasing the rainbow's end.' And so he settles down and learns not to expect too much and represses the part of himself which used, as he would say, to 'cry for the moon.'… But supposing infinite happiness really is there, waiting for us? Suppose one really could catch the rainbow's end? In that case it would be a pity to find out too late (a moment after death) that by our supposed 'common sense' we had stifled ourselves in the faculty of enjoying it.[5]

Then Lewis offers us a third Way, in one of the most famous passages he ever wrote. He suggests that this longing that nothing on earth can satisfy must be a natural desire (like our desire for food and drink and safety) rather than an artificial, socially constructed desire (like a desire for a new dress or a sports car), because it is common to all humanity; it is not the creation of society, advertising, or fiction. He writes:

> Creatures are not born with [natural] desires unless satisfaction for those desires exists. A baby feels hunger: well, there is such a thing as food. A duckling wants to swim: well, there is such a thing as water. Men feel sexual desire: well, there is such a thing as sex. If I find in myself a desire which no experience in this world can satisfy, the most probable explanation is that I was made for another world.

> If none of my earthly pleasures satisfy it, that does not prove that the universe is a fraud. Probably earthly pleasures were not meant to satisfy it, but only to arouse it, to suggest the real thing. If that is so, I must take care, on the one hand, never to despise, or be unthankful for, these earthly blessings, and on the other, never to mistake them for the something else of which they are only a kind of copy, or echo, or mirage. I must keep alive in myself the desire for my true country, which I shall not find till after death; I must never let it get snowed under or turned aside....

There is a subtle shift in this last quote, Krystal: you may have noticed it. In the others Lewis spoke about Joy as something that we experience only in rare, distinct, painful moments of longing for something that nothing on earth can ever satisfy—experiences often triggered within us by temporal manifestations of exquisite beauty in art or nature. But here he writes as if there is an underlying, inconsolable desire that forms the backdrop to almost *everything* we think we desire in this life. He explained this best in his book *The*

Problem of Pain, so I'll share this one last quote from Lewis with you before I close:

> There have been times I think we do not desire heaven; but more often I find myself wondering whether, in our heart of hearts, we have ever desired anything else. You may have noticed that the books you really love are bound together by a secret thread. You know very well what is the common quality that makes you love them, though you cannot put it into words: but most of your friends do not see it at all, and often wonder why, liking this, you should also like that. Again, you have stood before some landscape, which seems to embody what you have been looking for all your life; and then turned to the friend at your side who appears to be seeing what you saw—but at the first words a gulf yawns between you, and you realize that this landscape means something totally different to him, that he is pursuing an alien vision and cares nothing for the ineffable suggestion by which you are transported. Even in your hobbies, has there not always been some secret attraction which the others are curiously ignorant of—something not to be identified with, but always on the verge of breaking through, the smell of cut wood in the workshop, or the clap-clap of water against the boat's side? Are not all lifelong friendships born at the moment when at last you meet another human being who has some inkling (but faint and uncertain even in the best) of that something which you were born desiring, and which, beneath the flux of other desires and in all the momentary silences between the louder passions, night and day, year by year, from childhood to old age, you are looking for, watching for, listening for? You have never *had* it. All the things that have ever deeply possessed your soul have been but hints of it—tantalising glimpses, promises never quite fulfilled, echoes that died away just as they caught your ear. But if it should ever really become manifest—if there ever came an echo that did not die away but swelled into the sound itself—you would know it. Beyond all possibility of doubt you would say 'Here at last is the thing I was made for.' We cannot tell each other

about it. It is the secret signature of each soul, the incommunicable, unappeasable want, the thing we desired before we met our wives or made our friends or chose our work, and which we shall still desire on our deathbeds, when the mind no longer knows wife or friend or work. While we are, this is. If we lose this, we lose all.[6]

What is this nameless thing that we so desperately long for? What is this transcendent "something" which we desire so painfully when that desire is triggered by mere transient manifestations of beauty in this world? Lewis calls it "heaven." Krystal, you called it "home," the place we were made for, and "Valhalla," where the heroes find eternal rest. I think the ancient philosopher Boethius said it best: what we really long for is *the endless possession of perfect, boundless good.* We know very well that this is what we all want because no one would ever turn it down if freely offered, and it would leave no desire unsatisfied; our search and longing finally would be at an end. But what can "perfect, boundless (infinite) good" be other than God himself, the Infinitely Perfect Being? St. Augustine knew this. He wrote about 5 million words in his lifetime, but one sentence stands out among them all: "You made us for Yourself, Lord, and our hearts will never find rest until they rest in You."

So we have come to the door of the secret of the human heart, the "Secret Garden" within each one of us. We cannot flee from that door, try as we might. Even if we attempt to run away from it, He beckons us to come back, both in momentary stabs of Joy, and in the inconsolable desire hidden in all our desires.

The only question is: will we open the door and step in?

Love to you always,

Uncle Robert

6. A Message in the Stars

Hi Krystal,

You never told me before that you were taking a course in Physics this spring. Well, you are a brave soul indeed—especially for a World Literature and French major! I remember when I was a college student, although utterly terrified of mathematics and the sciences I had to take a few courses in those departments to graduate. So I decided to take one entitled "Physics for Poets." From the title it sounded like it would be "right up my alley." In the end I got a C-minus; in other words, I barely made it out alive!

It's great that your Physics professor is not afraid to discuss "big questions" in class such as "Why is there such a high degree of order in the universe rather than sheer chaos?" Of course, that's really a philosophical question rather than one that can be answered by the natural sciences alone. Scientists can only tell us how nature operates, I mean what laws can be formulated to describe how the fundamental particles and forces in the universe behave. They cannot really tell us why nature behaves according to one particular set of laws rather than another set, or indeed, why nature obeys any "laws" at all. Science asks what the order of nature is and how it works; Philosophy asks why there is any order in nature in the first place.

That seems to be the question that most intrigues you, Krystal. And it's not a "high-brow" question at all. It's the same question that any little child begins to ask when he looks at the sun rising in the morning or hears the wind rustle the leaves and asks: "Why?" The child is not usually asking just "How does it work"? He's asking what the purpose is, what it's all for. "The sun rises in the morning, my son, so we can have warmth and light to grow our food, and do our work, and see with our eyes this beautiful world in which we live."

That's the kind of answer children really seek, because the mind and heart of a child naturally doubts that the order he perceives in the world is all simply random and meaningless. The child wants to know the design and purpose of things—and one day may ask if there is Designer and Giver-of-Purpose to the whole show.

You were entirely right when you reminded me of what I said to you in my first letter: that we can stand on the solid ground of common sense realities ("properly basic beliefs") and on that basis "reach for the heavens." This is a good case in point. *There is a high degree of order and regularity in the universe that seems to achieve (at least temporarily) various purposes—that's obvious to anyone who carefully observes the natural world—and this kind of intricate order implies the existence of an Intelligent Designer.*

Let's consult the philosophy of St. Thomas Aquinas again. In his two greatest works, he argued this way: we all observe that in nature material things of very different types seem to cooperate to produce and maintain a relatively stable cosmic order. The behavior of all these material things harmonizes in such a way as to achieve that end or purpose. Most of the things that work together in nature to achieve this goal, however, are *non-intelligent material things*: in other words, they don't have minds that can consciously envision this purpose and intentionally carry it out. *This unconscious cooperation of many different kinds of material things in the production and maintenance of a fairly stable, intelligible world order simply cries out for an explanation.* St. Thomas argues that the most likely explanation for this feature of the natural universe is that *there is a supernatural Power and Intelligence who is the author of this world-order, and who maintains it with at least that basic purpose in view.*

The best analogy I can think of is a symphony orchestra. Notice that a symphony orchestra is made up of a combination of intelligent and non-intelligent material things: the musicians, of course, but also their instruments, music stands, sheets of music, the chairs they sit on, etc. And yet, all these intelligent and non-intelligent things somehow work together to play a recognizably unified and orderly piece of music. Why is that possible? Only because someone intelligent wrote a common score of music for the musicians to play—the performance of that common music was the purpose the composer evidently had in view from the start—and only because all are directed to play that common music by one conductor. On this analogy, the Composer-Conductor, of course, is God.

Our friend Rodney Holder has a good summary of the situation:

> If there is no God then we are expected to believe that the orderliness in the universe, manifested in all matter at all times and in all places obeying the same set of laws, is a brute, unexplained fact; and this seems extremely unlikely. Conversely, such order is extremely likely if it derives from a common source, just in the way that all tenpenny pieces are identical because they all come from the same mould. Thus, order is very likely if there is a God. Moreover, if God produces a universe at all he is very likely to produce an orderly one because of his character [as supremely Intelligent and Good]….There is much more likely to be order of this kind if there is a God than if there is not.[1]

In other words; a high degree of order and design in the universe is precisely what we should expect if there is a God of Infinite Intelligence and Power behind it all, but not what we would expect if there is not, and if everything is the way it is merely by chance.

I am glad that your Physics professor told you about the scientific evidence for cosmic design that scientists have discovered in recent decades: its further corroboration of the argument for an Intelligent Designer. Philosopher Peter Kreeft sums it up as follows in an article on his website (Kreeft, by the way, is an excellent and easy-to-understand philosopher, from Boston College). This quote may help you wrap-your-head-around the subject:

> Another especially strong aspect of the design argument is the so-called *anthropic principle*, according to which the universe seems to have been specially designed from the beginning for human life to evolve. If the temperature of the primal fireball that resulted from the Big Bang some fifteen to twenty billion years ago, which was the beginning of our universe, had been a trillionth of a degree colder or hotter, the carbon molecule that is the foundation of all organic life could never have developed…. Sounds suspiciously like a plot. If the cosmic rays had bombarded the primordial slime [on planet earth] at a slightly different angle or time or intensity, the hemoglobin molecule, necessary for all warm-blooded animals, could never have evolved. The chance of this molecule evolving is something like one in a trillion trillion.[2]

Some physicists describe such improbable cosmic events (and there are dozens of them) as "anthropic coincidences." In short, the natural universe as a whole seems to manifest a high degree of "fine-tuning": in other words, it manifests a purpose behind it to provide the conditions necessary for the existence and survival of creatures just like us. Surely, it is highly unlikely that all this "fine-tuning" is just the result of chance or accident!

Atheist philosopher A.C. Grayling remains unimpressed by the "fine-tuning" argument. At the end of a chapter of his book *The God Argument* he writes:

> The fact that we exist because of how things happen to be with the universe's structure and properties entails nothing about design or purpose. Depending on your point of view, it is just a lucky or unlucky result of how things happen to be. The universe's parameters are not *tuned on purpose for us to exist*. It is the other way around: we exist because the laws happen to be as they are.[3]

Grayling compares the situation with the main "coincidences" down through history that resulted in the birth of you and me. For example, for you and me to exist as the unique individuals that we are required certain people in the past (our ancestors) deciding to marry each other and raise children, and others deciding to immigrate to new lands to escape war and death, etc. "If my forebears had been inconsiderate enough to do other things in other ways," Grayling remarks, "I would not be marveling now at how fine-tuned history was in bringing it about that I exist. I do not, however, think that I was the point and purpose of all these events, however lucky for me."[4]

Grayling's comparison, however, misses the mark. The circumstances that resulted in the births of you and me, Krystal, are the result of the free-will decisions (who decided to marry who, etc.) of *many* intelligent agents down through history. It stands to reason that our particular births were not pre-meditated by *them*. But the fashioning of the natural laws and properties of the universe from the beginning in such a remarkable way that any human life could exist anywhere at all in this universe can be explained by the actions of just One Intelligent Agent: namely, God. What other likely explanation could there be?

Besides, Grayling has not answered the fine-tuning argument: he has merely side-stepped it. He ignores the vital things that scientists have learned about what "just happens" to enable life to exist at all in this universe. It's not that two or three unlikely factors happened to coincide to make this happen. The fact is that there was a confluence of dozens of initial conditions in place right from the start, from the Big Bang onward: all of them needed for life to happen anywhere at all in the universe, and each one of them infinitesimally improbable in itself—not to mention the improbability of all of these factors occurring at once. The intricacy, improbability, and remarkable result of this initial cosmic "blueprint"—namely, creatures like us—is surely more likely to be the product of a purposeful, Intelligent Agent than of sheer chance.

I like Dinesh D'Souza's summary of the situation: "Fine-tuning [of our universe] is much less likely than the odds of me buying a lottery ticket in all fifty states and winning every time. How clueless do you have to be to fail to recognize that something very strange is going on here?"[5]

Still, a skeptic may ask: "Isn't it at least *possible* that all this intricate order and design in nature happened by chance, without a Designer?" Maybe so; it's remotely possible, but who would rely on a remotely possible explanation for all this when a simpler and more probable explanation is near at hand: a single Intelligent Designer. Peter Kreeft asks us to imagine finding the huge letters "S.O.S" written in the sand on a beach. Of course, it is remotely possible—perhaps a one-in-a-trillion-trillion chance—that those letters were formed by the random blowing of sand in the wind. But a possible explanation is not the same as a probable one; who would ever cling to that one-in-a-trillion-trillion explanation when there is a simpler and more obvious one: an intelligent agent had been there, someone intelligent enough to design and write the message.

In fact, the "message" spelled out in the natural universe for all to see seems to be written, at least in part, in the language of mathematics. World famous physicist Paul A. M. Dirac, for example, has observed that "God is a mathematician of a very high order, and He used advanced mathematics in constructing the universe."[6] And here is Einstein again:

> I am not an atheist, and I don't think I can call myself a pantheist. We are in the position of a little child entering a huge library filled with books in many languages. The child knows someone must have written those books. It does not know how. It does not understand the languages in which they are written. The child dimly suspects a mysterious order

in the arrangement of the books but doesn't know what it is. That, it seems to me, is the attitude of even the most intelligent human being toward God. We see the universe marvelously arranged and obeying certain laws but only dimly understand these laws. Our limited minds grasp the mysterious force that moves the constellations.[7]

Of course, someone in your physics class might object to this by pointing to the findings of quantum physics. Scientists now believe there is indeed an element of "randomness" or "unpredictability" throughout the natural universe at the most microscopic level. Electrons, for example, do not always behave according to rigid natural laws; their behavior only "averages out" to produce a general order on a larger scale. Still, the fact that their behavior does average-out, in all places and all times, to produce a relatively stable and uniform natural order, is a remarkable thing. It's precisely what we mean by nature as a whole manifesting a high degree of order and purpose that cries out for an explanation.

Besides, the case for an Intelligent Designer does not depend upon the natural universe being *perfectly* orderly in every respect, like a perfect machine. Remember our symphony orchestra analogy: even if some of the instruments miss a note on occasion, or some of the chairs on which the musicians are seated "squeak" a bit, and even though the music won't last forever, it is still the case that the orchestra is playing a recognizably ordered and designed piece of music. It is still very likely that they are able to do so because some Intelligent Agent composed that common piece for them to play.

Back in the 18th century the philosopher David Hume came up with another objection to the argument for an Intelligent Designer. It's worth considering here, Krystal, in case someone brings it up in your discussions. Hume said that the only reason we conclude that certain kinds of order and design we find in the world are the products of "intelligent designers" is that we have actually experienced—I mean, seen with our own eyes, or know others we can trust who have seen with their own eyes—intelligent designers making those very kinds of things. So, for example, if we find a watch, we conclude that it was made by an intelligent being, a watchmaker, not only because it has an intricate design, but also because we know from our experience, or from the experience of others, that that particular kind of orderly thing—a watch—is produced by watchmakers. Similarly, we conclude that an "S.O.S." written in letters in the sand was probably produced by an intelligent being, a human being, because we know from our experience that human beings write messages in letters. No one, however, has ever seen or experienced a god making a world, so we do not really know if an intricately ordered universe as a whole is the kind of thing that only a god can produce or is likely to produce, or if there is some other more probable cause for cosmic order.

Hume is right: no one has ever seen an intelligent god making a world. Nevertheless, there are aspects of the world in which we live that provide us with a close analogy, a microcosm, a good "snapshot" of the universe as a whole. If intricate order and "fine-tuning" in the microcosm comes from an intelligent designer, then it is reasonable to assume that the same applies to the whole cosmos. Again, take my symphony orchestra analogy; it's like a little microcosm, a snapshot of the universe as a whole. And it shows what we all know to be true: *that in reality as we know it, intricate, stable, pervasive and purpose-achieving order is the kind of thing produced by intelligent agents.*

However, Hume is not beaten yet. He claims that he can give us close analogies for the universe as a whole that do not require an Intelligent Designer behind it all. For example, he says, the universe can be compared to a single living organism, like a plant. Plants have an intricate, stable and pervasive order, yet they organize their own cells, nourish and reproduce themselves without need for an Intelligent Designer to get involved.

But Hume's analogy will not do. For the order and design of plants certainly does not explain itself. Plants, if you will, play the score of music written for them, but they did not write it! They obey the natural laws written for them, just as everything else in the world does.

"Ah yes," you might say, "but it is the impersonal mechanism of evolution—the laws of genetic mutation and natural selection ("survival of the fittest")—that is what designed plants and animals to be the way they are, not any supernatural Intelligent Agent."

But this will not do either. First of all, evolution remains an unproven scientific theory, and actually contradicts much of the fossil record that we have. Second, as the leaders of the new "Intelligent Design" movement in science have demonstrated, there are many aspects of living organisms that the mechanisms of gradual, step by step evolution could never explain: the "irreducible complexity" of many living organs, for example, and even of the simplest cell. Only an Intelligent Agent could create such things. (If you can, Krystal, get a hold of a copy of a book I co-edited with scientist Paul Brown entitled *More Than Myth?* where Intelligent Design theory is clearly explained).

For example, in *The Way of the Cell*, biologist Franklin Harold has shown that each living cell is like a factory in itself, and far more integrated and complex than any factory, or even any super-computer, that human beings can make today. "Indeed," he writes, "cell components as we know them are so thoroughly integrated that one can scarcely imagine how any one function could have arisen in the absence of others…. [Cells] break down food-stuffs, extract energy, manufacture precursors, assemble constituents, note and execute genetic instructions, and keep all this frantic activity coordinated."[8]

Dinesh D'Souza asks the obvious question about all of this:

> So how did we get cells? Darwin did not even attempt an answer to this question. He recognized that there was no way to explain the integrated functionality of the cell by appealing to evolution or natural selection. Evolution itself presumes and requires cells that come fully formed with the capacity for metabolism and self-replication. No reproduction, no natural selection. Clearly, the basic template of life came fully formed when life first appeared on this earth 4 billion years ago.[9]

Third, even if these difficulties can be overcome, and evolution is in fact a sufficient explanation for the nature and variety of living creatures that we find on this planet, still, the process of evolution itself would be another expression of order and design in the universe. Ask yourself: why would our world as a whole be equipped with an intricate, stable, and pervasive evolutionary system, rather than some other system of laws of biological development—or none at all? It may have elements of chance involved in it—random genetic mutations, and so on—but even these elements somehow work within the system to help churn out creatures of ever higher levels of complexity and survival capability. The progressive advance of life on this planet is surely evidence of design embedded in nature. In any case, an evolutionary system is not sheer chaos: it is part of what we call "the natural order."

Besides, as we have already discussed, Krystal (in our previous correspondence), the natural order of material things (matter and energy, atoms and molecules) cannot account for the mystery of the human spirit, with its capacities for rational thought, free choice, and longing for the Infinite Good. So no analogies for the universe as a whole based on mere plant or animal life can be called "close analogies," or good "snapshots" of our world as a whole. In short, Hume's argument just doesn't work.

One more challenge to belief in an Intelligent Designer comes from contemporary physics. Some physicists today will argue that perhaps there is not just one universe (namely, our own), but billions and trillions of universes as yet unknown to us. Perhaps universes are giving rise to new universes all the time. Those universes each would have their own unique features, and their own degree of order or chaos built in. If so, it is bound to happen, even just by chance, that at least one of those universes would have the high degree of order and design that we see in our universe—and so, in this way the order and design of our universe could be explained without reference to any supernatural Intelligent Designer.

This is a simplified version of what is known as the "Multiverse" hypothesis. The details are incredibly complex. But you don't need to muck around with the scientific details to realize that something is wrong with the philosophical reasoning here. For even if it is possible that universes can give rise to the existence of other universes through the operation of the most fundamental principles of quantum physics, and even if that explains how our own universe came to be one of trillions, *that still would not explain why the multiverse obeys this particular set of laws of universe-creation rather than some other set, or none at all. Where did these common, basic laws of universe-creation come from?* This degree of intricate, stable and pervasive order in the multiverse—of a kind that ultimately churned out an amazing universe like our own—would still cry out for an explanation; and the best explanation for such design is still an Intelligent Designer.

Besides, at the moment we know for sure of the existence of only one universe: our own. To appeal to the merely *possible* existence of trillions of universes to account for order and design in our own universe, rather than to the existence of one supernatural Intelligent Designer, seems the height of absurdity. It postulates the existence of trillions of factors to account for something, when one, simple, sufficient explanation will do. It's the kind of mental gymnastics that people get into when they are desperately trying to run away from something—or in this case, from Someone.

Krystal, I know you have a favorite quote from Oscar Wilde: "We are all in the gutter, but some of us are looking at the stars." Fantastic: It's so true! But what do we see when we look at the stars? A beauty so deep that sometimes it makes us long for something transcendent, something that nothing on earth can satisfy? You bet—that's what the Romantics would say, and they were right. But the Rationalists see something else too, a message written in the stars which I have been sharing with you in this letter. It's all summed up in the closing lines of Joseph Addison's famous 18th century poem (have you ever read it?)—so with this I will close:

What though in solemn silence all
Move round the dark terrestrial ball,
What though no real voice, nor sound,
Amidst their radiant orbs be found;
In reason's ear they all rejoice,
And utter forth a glorious voice,
Forever singing as they shine,
"The hand that made us is divine."

With Love,

Uncle Robert

7. The Inner Light

Dear Krystal,

So, in your World Literature major you have found a "favorite author" after all: Leo Tolstoy! Russian novelists are indeed a fascinating bunch, and of course, Tolstoy is one of the great masters. I am glad you liked *Anna Karenina* so much, and that now you are digging into that collection of Tolstoy's short stories that I gave you for your birthday (just bear in mind that for Tolstoy a "short" story can be about 100 pages long!). If you survive reading all 800 pages of War and Peace some day (I've never done it), then you can truly count yourself a Tolstoy fan!

It strikes me that you were bound to love Tolstoy because it's in your "blood-stream." Your Mom and Dad may have told you this already, but the "Stackpole" side of the family is actually descended from Ohio Quakers, and the Quaker tradition is in many ways a fore-runner of Tolstoy. The founder of the Quakers in Great Britain, George Fox, taught them to seek the "inner Light" of God within themselves and within every person, primarily through silent prayer and radical simplicity of life. The Quakers were especially moved by those passages in the Bible that speak of this divine "Light": "the light that lightens every man that comes into the world" (Jn 1:9). They believed that this inner Light can be trusted to show us how to live, and how to find the same Light within the hearts of others. It is expressed in the Bible in the prayer to God that "in Thy light we may see light" (Ps 36:9). As a result, the Quaker colony in early Pennsylvania, as you may know, became a center of religious tolerance, and opposition to war and slavery.

Tolstoy's philosophy of life is very similar. As you will see from some of his short stories, Tolstoy believed that within each one of us, even those whose hearts are hardened by worldliness and corruption, there shines an inner Light that beckons us always to do good, to love our neighbors as ourselves, and to trust in that Light, even in the midst of darkness and death. Read especially his stories *The Death of Ivan Illych* and *Master and Man.* They are great examples of how the Light within calls people out of their shallow and self-centered existence, especially when the approach of death wakes them up from moral and spiritual slumber. As you know already from your study of his life, Tolstoy became an ardent pacifist and a vocal defender of religious liberty. He also tried to live as the Russian peasants did, in great simplicity. Much like the Quakers, Tolstoy believed that the pursuit of wealth and worldly honors can only be a distraction from deep listening and attentiveness to the inner Light.

This is part of my soul and my "blood-stream" too, Krystal. To my mind, most of it is profoundly "true as far as it goes," and the world would be a lot better place if there were more people who followed such beliefs. However, over the years I came to see that, beautiful and idealistic as it is, there are very important truths about human life, and about God, that Tolstoy and the Quakers leave out. As a religious worldview, it now seems woefully incomplete to me. For example, how many people really turn their lives around and attain a settled love for truth and goodness thru the beckoning of the *inner* Light alone? As creatures lost in the dark wilderness of *outer* things, possessed by desires for popularity and worldly success, wealth and comfort, sex and romance, social status and political correctness, we need a Light that does more than just flicker like a dying candle within our souls. Only a Light that can come to our rescue by seeking us out in our outer world of flesh—our joys, pains and sorrows—can really meet us there, right where we are lost, and lead us home.

Tolstoy is fantastic in describing all the things that possess and destroy the human soul. He's a master psychologist! But he never really convinces me that he has uncovered the secret of what can rescue the soul from the darkness.

Still, I mustn't "throw the baby out with the bathwater." To some extent I think Tolstoy and the Quakers are absolutely right: there is indeed in each one of us an inner Light, even as the Bible says. The philosopher Immanuel Kant put it well: "Two things fill the mind with new and ever increasing admiration and awe... the starry heavens above me and the moral law within me." In my last letter I said something to you about the message of "the starry heavens above." In this one—since I have some time to kill, and since you are diving into Tolstoy now—I'll share a few thoughts about the inner Light: the inner voice of conscience that calls us all to do good.

In his book *Mere Christianity*, C.S. Lewis claims that every human heart contains some basic moral principles: standards of benevolence, self-control, fairness, and courage, for example. In accordance with the classical philosophical tradition he calls these ethical standards "The Law of Human Nature." Lewis explains:

> When the older thinkers called the Law of Right and Wrong 'the Law of Nature,' they really meant the Law of Human Nature. The idea was that just as all bodies are governed by the law of gravitation, and organisms by biological laws, so the creature called man also had his law—with this great difference, that a body could not choose whether it obeyed the law of gravitation or not, but a man could choose either to obey the Law of Human Nature or to disobey it.[1]

In other words, the Law of Human Nature, or "the Natural Moral Law," tells us how we "ought" to live if we are to be *truly and fully human*—to fulfill our Creator's design, and fit in with the natural harmony of things—but it does not compel us to live that way. We might choose to live otherwise.

Another way to think of it is this: remember how I wrote to you a few months ago that everyone has a desire for the endless possession of perfect, boundless Good? If C.S. Lewis is right, our heart's desire is not just to see that Infinite Good, not just to know about it, but to participate in it somehow, to "bathe" in it: one day to reach a *complete union* of mind and heart, body and soul with it, immersed in that ocean of Good. Well, if the Light within us is this Light of perfect boundless Good, the Divine Light, He must be shining in our hearts to help us fulfill that desire; He must be drawing us to seek the best way to *reflect* His Infinite Light in our own finite, limited, human form of being. In short, He evidently wants us to let His Light shine *through* us—each one in his own unique way, through our unique personalities and life circumstances. That would be about as close as we could come—in this life, at any rate—to the complete union with Him that we long for.

The question naturally arises: "But how do we know that this Natural Moral Law really comes from God? Maybe it was just put into each one of us by society: by our education and upbringing."

No doubt societies often endorse, and even enforce aspects of the Natural Moral Law, for the common good. If the Natural Moral Law was merely a social invention, however, then we would expect there to be radically different moral codes from one civilization to the next, just as there are radically different standards of fashion in clothing. But such is not the case. C.S. Lewis shows that at least the basic moral principles within every human heart are cross-cultural: they are not merely the separate invention of each society to keep its members in-line. Lewis writes:

> I know that some people say the idea of a Law of Nature or decent behavior known to all men is unsound, because different civilizations have had quite different moralities.

But this is not true. There have been differences between their moralities, but these have never amounted to anything like a total difference. If anyone will take the trouble to compare the moral teaching of, say, the ancient Egyptians, Babylonians, Hindus, Chinese, Greeks and Romans, what will really strike him will be how very like they are to each other and to our own. Some of the evidence for this I have put together in the appendix of another book called *The Abolition of Man*; but for our present purpose I need only ask the reader to think what a totally different morality would mean. Think of a country where people were admired for running away in battle, or where a man felt proud of double-crossing all the people who had been kindest to him. You might just as well try to imagine a country where two and two made five. Men have differed as regards what people you ought to be unselfish to—whether it was only your own family, or your fellow countrymen, or every one. But they have always agreed you ought not to put yourself first. Selfishness has never been admired. Men have differed as to whether you should have one wife or four. But they have always agreed that you must not simply have any woman you liked….

It seems, then, we are forced to believe in a real [universal standard of] Right and Wrong. People may be sometimes mistaken about them, just as people sometimes get their sums wrong; but they are not a matter of mere taste and opinion any more than the multiplication table.[2]

Thus, for Lewis this common core of moral values cries out for an explanation. Simply put: a universal Natural Moral Law points toward the existence of a universal Moral Lawgiver who fashioned nature itself:

I find that I do not exist on my own, that I am under a law; that somebody or something wants me to behave in a certain way….

The position of the question, then, is like this. We want to know whether the universe simply happens to be what it is for no reason or whether there is a power behind it that makes it what it is…. If there was a controlling power outside the universe, it could not show itself to us as one of the facts inside the universe—no more than an architect of a house could actually be a wall or staircase or fireplace in that house. The only way in which we could expect it to show itself would be inside ourselves as an influence or command trying to get us to behave in a certain way [in harmony with its plan for the whole house]. And that is just what we do find inside ourselves. Surely that should arouse our suspicions? In the only case where you can expect to get an answer, the answer turns out to be Yes….[3]

At this point, however, an Evolutionist may object. He might say: "I can give you a better reason for the common core of moral beliefs that we find in all the civilizations of the world: the common need for survival. Human beings have a biological survival instinct with which we have been equipped by evolution. As a result we instinctively know that certain kinds of behavior are destructive of ourselves, our families, our particular societies, and of the human race as a whole. The more enlightened ones among us—driven by this same instinct, but applying our intelligence in accord with it— realize that survival of the species as a whole, and of the whole biosphere on which we depend, has to take priority or we are all doomed. So the common light is not a supernatural Light, not Light from a divine Moral Lawgiver, but simply our survival instinct, the biological imperative in our genes to survive and flourish."

Let's look at this more closely, Krystal, because it is "trendy" at colleges and universities to think about the Natural Moral Law in this way. Altruism, they say, is simply rooted in the biological survival instinct. I see two big problems here.

First, if such is the case, why would we be justified in thinking that we "ought" to survive more than weasels or jellyfish? Just because we have an instinct that tells us we should? But every living creature has the same survival instinct; so what makes us so special? On the one hand, the human spirit has an extraordinary capacity for creativity, wisdom, and love (remember our discussions about the dignity of the human spirit a few months ago?). On the other hand, given the past record of human behavior—our capacity for rapacious abuse of the natural environment, for murder and exploitation, the invention of weapons of mass destruction, etc. one could make a fair argument that the best chance for life on our planet to survive would be to get rid of the human race as soon as possible!

Believers in the universal Moral Lawgiver, however, have a clear answer to this dilemma. If a supernatural Creator, the Infinite Light, shines within our hearts the light of the Natural Moral Law, then we know that humanity is meant to survive and flourish as part of His purpose for the universe He made. According to that Law, the highest moral principle is not our biological survival—for we should never corrupt the immortal souls of men and women to achieve it—but it is certainly a very good thing, above the survival of any other creature. All living creatures have a survival instinct, but we know we "ought" to protect and nurture human life more than the lives of weasels and jellyfish, if it comes to that, because there is something of special value about human beings: we are embodied, immortal spirits. Our Creator has reminded us of that, thru the Natural Moral Law He shines within us.

Second, if the biological survival of our species is really the highest moral principle, what kind of overall moral code would that leave us with? No doubt it would give us something like the code of 19th century philosophers like John Stuart Mill: what is right is simply "the greatest good for the greatest number of people"—for the greatest number of people would surely benefit most by the long term survival and flourishing of the human race as a whole. It's known as the "Utilitarian" principle. And as most ethicists know, it is fraught with difficulties. The most atrocious human rights abuses can be justified on this basis, for it is reasoning beloved by tyrants, world conquerors, and terrorists alike: "To make an omelet, you have to crack a few eggs."

The Utilitarian can say: "Sure, exterminating the inferior races, the senile, the terminally ill, and the handicapped is distasteful, but if it is needed to enable the human race as a whole to survive and flourish in the long run, how can anyone object that it is unjust or immoral? It's only the application of the natural, evolutionary principle of 'the survival of the fittest.' For the human race to have the best long-range chance of survival, it needs to be maximally fit. Only the unfit, the drag on the human race, the 'useless eaters' will be terminated. The vast majority of the human race will be better off as a result, for centuries to come!" Again, a Utilitarian can say: "It may be a regrettable necessity that we have to fly airplanes into the World Trade Center and kill thousands of innocent people in the process, but if it promotes the destruction of corrupt western society and its replacement with a far better one, an Islamic world order, in the long run it's all worth it!" Again, "It may be temporarily necessary to send all of the bourgeois capitalist sympathizers off to be 're-educated' in gulags in Siberia, but if it effectively serves the establishment of the ideal socialist state, and the spread of the best global society, world socialism, it is surely the right thing to do!"

Of course, the great teachers of morality have never reasoned about right and wrong in such a way. Jesus of Nazareth, Socrates, Cicero, Lao-Tse, Buddha—whatever their differences may have been, they did not see human lives merely as instruments for a better future for the human species as a whole. Rather, they taught that each and every human life has value in itself, with a spiritual dimension and a divinely given purpose: to live in the Light of the Natural

Moral Law, each in his own unique way. Unless you are going to sweep aside the teachings of all of them as so many ethical "dinosaurs," you have to admit that the common moral wisdom of the human race stands against the idea that the highest principle of all is simply the biological survival of our species.

In short, the common, inner Light does not seem to be reducible to "nothing but" our biological survival instinct, and "enlightened" moral reflection in the service of it ("Nothing Buttery" again!). Evolution cannot explain this mystery: belief in a common Moral Lawgiver can.

There is another, very curious thing about the Natural Moral Law: whatever we perceive that Moral Law to be, we know we "ought" to follow it, and follow it absolutely. It has the highest, unconditional claim upon us. People may disagree in conscience about the right thing to do—but whatever they perceive to be right, their conscience tells them they ought to do it, no matter what.

You might be a moral "relativist." In other words, you might think to yourself: "What's right for me is right for me, and what's right for you is right for you—no common Moral Law should bind us" (a self-contradictory statement, by the way: for the relativist presumably wants the rest of the world to live by the same principle!). In any case, if you honestly believe that is the best principle to live by, then you know you "ought" to live by it if you are to have any integrity at all. You know you ought to follow your conscience (even if, without realizing it, your conscience is misinformed!): for the voice of conscience is always binding; it always makes an absolute claim upon each one of us, and often plagues us with guilt when we fall short.

This is very strange, Krystal, when you think about it. Philosopher Peter Kreeft writes:

> Modern people often say they believe that there are no
> universally binding moral obligations, that we must all follow

our own private conscience…. Now where did conscience get such an absolute authority—an authority admitted even by the moral subjectivist and relativist?[4]

Such an absolute, unconditional claim on our loyalty can only come from an Absolute Source. But where do we find such a Source? I am certainly not an Absolute Being myself: I am often confused, often unreliable, and only a temporary resident of planet earth, "here today and gone tomorrow." Nor is society or humanity as a whole an Absolute Being, for the same could be said about them. Nor is nature itself an Absolute Being, for it too had a beginning and will one day have an end. Besides, nature is not really "superior" to me, for at least I have an immaterial, immortal soul, and nature does not; and at least I can comprehend in my soul the Natural Moral Law, and nature cannot. Peter Kreeft concludes:

> The only source of absolute moral obligation left is someone superior to me. This binds my will morally, with rightful demands for complete obedience.

> Thus God, or something like God, is the only adequate source and ground for the absolute moral obligation we all feel to obey our conscience. Conscience is thus explainable only as the voice of God in the soul.[5]

This idea that conscience is "the voice of God in the soul" certainly fits with what conscience feels like when we experience its claim upon us. The best description I have ever read of this comes from the 19th century Catholic writer John Henry Newman;

> If, as is the case, we feel responsibility, are ashamed, are frightened, at transgressing the voice of conscience, this implies that there is One to whom we are responsible, before whom we are ashamed, whose claims upon us we fear. If, on

doing wrong, we feel the same tearful, brokenhearted sorrow which overwhelms us in hurting a mother; if on doing right we enjoy the same sunny serenity of mind, the same soothing satisfactory delight which follows on receiving praise from a father, we certainly have within us the image of some person, to whom our love and veneration look, in whose smile we find our happiness, for whom we yearn, to whom we direct our pleadings, in whose anger we are troubled and waste away. These feelings are such as require for their exciting cause an intelligent being; we are not affectionate towards a stone, nor do we feel shame before a horse or a dog; we have no remorse or compunction upon breaking mere human law; yet, so it is, conscience excites all these painful emotions, confusion, foreboding, self-condemnation; and on the other hand, it sheds upon us a deep peace, a sense of security, a resignation, and a hope, which there is no sensible, no earthly object to elicit. "The wicked flees when no one pursueth;" then why does he flee? Whence his terror? Who is it that he sees in solitude, in darkness, in the hidden chambers of his heart? If the cause of these emotions does not belong to this visible world, the object towards which his perception is directed must be Supernatural and Divine.[6]

Well, Krystal, isn't that in the end what the Quakers, and Tolstoy, and C.S. Lewis were all trying to say? Within each one of us there is the same inner Light, the same inner Voice, beckoning us to do good and shun evil, and making an absolute, unconditional claim upon our loyalty. Whose Voice could this be other than the Voice of the Absolute Being who made us?

Love always,

Uncle Robert

8. The New Age, and Other Options

Dear Krystal,

Finally, some good "push-back."

Over the last few months I have shared with you many of my own philosophical reflections and ramblings, all of which you have graciously received. But I know how bright you are, and I wondered if, all the while, some tough questions were brewing in your mind. Now I see that they were!

Be assured that your questions are *excellent* ones (anyway, I expected nothing less from my brilliant niece, who is an honest seeker of the truth). I will do my best to respond to them. I wish I had a quick and easy answer for everything, but, alas, you are in dialogue with me, I'm afraid, and not with a Thomas Aquinas or an Albert Einstein!

I'll take your three main questions in the order that you sent them to me.

1) "Couldn't everything that you wrote to support the existence of a supernatural Creator and the human spirit have an even better explanation? I mean, suppose there is a spiritual realm, but it consists not of God and individual souls, but of one World-Soul who fills the whole universe, and the physical universe is just His body. What we think of as our own individual selves could just be manifestations of that one World-Soul. (I am not making this up: we read about a similar perspective when we covered the 19th century American poets Emerson and Holmes). Anyway, this kind of God would be much closer to us than the transcendent, supernatural God of Christianity: we would be part of Him, included in His being, and not separated from Him. As well, if the natural world was seen by everyone as God's body, then we would be more likely to preserve and respect it, rather than destroying the environment, as we are doing now."

The theory you suggest, Krystal, is not just found in 19th century poetry: it's very close to what many in the "New Age" movement propose today. We can call it a form of "pantheism" or "panentheism" (meaning "everything is God," or "everything is a part of God"). At first glance, as you say, it makes God seem closer to us than a supernatural Being who is completely distinct from the world. Still, I think this feeling is misleading; it rests upon a misunderstanding of the Creator's relationship with His creation. From the perspective of classical Philosophy, God is not "separate," if by that you mean "aloof" in some way from His creatures. God is present everywhere: He holds his creatures in being at every moment, and knows everything about them. As St. Bernard of Clairvaux put it, He is "nearer to us than we are to ourselves." According to the Bible, "The Lord is good to all, and his compassion is over all that he has made" (Ps 145:9). St. Paul said it best in the Acts of the Apostles:

> He gives to all men life and breath and everything…that they should seek God in the hope that they might feel after him and find him. Yet he is not far from each one of us, for "In him we live and move and have our being;" as even some of your poets have said, "for we are indeed his offspring." (Acts 17: 27-28)

If we go further than this, Krystal, and say that the Creator is not only near to us with His power, knowledge, and benevolence, but we are actually *part of him, included in his being*—our souls part of his soul, and our bodies part of his body—then we may feel as if he is nearer to us, when in fact, he is farther away.

For one thing, he could not truly love us. After all, how could God be said to love me if he is me? Presumably, love means to care for another. It means to selflessly devote oneself to the good of others, like a mother caring for her children, or a firefighter rushing into a burning building to save someone's life. But the god of the New Age movement cannot be devoted to the good of others, because there are no "others"—there is only him. At best his concern for us would be a kind of enlightened self-interest, like someone who takes proper care of his own body by daily exercise. But that's not selfless concern for the needs of others, that's just prudent care for oneself. In short, the New Age god cannot really "love" his creation with selfless generosity, for nothing exists but his own self.

Moreover, if our souls are only parts or aspects of this one World-Soul, then the thoughts which I think in my head are not really my thoughts at all, but his. That contradicts our deepest intuitions, because we certainly experience our thoughts as if they were really our own. In addition, it contradicts what Descartes demonstrated (go back to my first letter); for if you say I am suffering from the illusion that I exist as a thinking self, still, there must be a thinking self here who is being deceived. In other words, it is self-evident, a "properly basic" belief that I am a real thinking self who thinks his own thoughts!

Furthermore, if there is one World-Soul, thinking all thoughts through all heads, why does he think contradictory thoughts in different people's heads? I mean, why does the World-Soul think in me that Fords are better than Toyotas, and in you think the opposite? Why in one mind is capitalism the best economic system and socialism is better to another—if there is really only one Mind? In short, the idea of a World-Soul is a poetic day-dream that just doesn't fit with reality.

Finally, you have to ask: what happens to the concept of moral value if there is nothing outside of God? How can we distinguish between good and evil, right and wrong, if everything—every situation, every human will, and every choice that is made—is a manifestation of the divine? C.S. Lewis once wrote:

If you do not take the distinction between good and bad very seriously, then it is easy to say that anything you find in this world is part of God. But of course, if you think some things really bad, and God really good, then you cannot talk like that. You must believe that God is separate from the world and that some of the things we see in it are contrary to His will. Confronted with cancer or a slum, a Pantheist can say, 'If only you would realize that this also is God.' The Christian....thinks God made the world—that space and time, heat and cold, all the colours and tastes, and all the animals and vegetables are things that God 'made up out of His head,' as a man makes up a story. But... a great many things have gone wrong with the world that God made and God insists, and insists very loudly, on our putting them right again.[1]

By the way, Krystal, I fully agree with you that one of those things that has gone terribly wrong is humanity's relationship with our natural environment. If there is a real Creator-God of infinite power, wisdom, and goodness, then He must have made the world according to a wise design. Everything that exists belongs to Him, fashioned in just the right way to serve His good purposes. Human beings are meant to be stewards of all that He has entrusted to us—and surely not to wantonly destroy it. In other words, Krystal, you don't have to be a pantheist to be a responsible environmentalist. You just have to be humble before the Creator of all.

2) "Couldn't someone just say that all your arguments for the existence of a Creator and for the human spirit are just expressions of wishful thinking? That is what the novelist Iris Murdoch would say. Maybe people just want to have the psychological comfort of religious beliefs. They desperately want to see themselves as creatures with a spirit that can live forever, and to live in a universe governed by a good God, and so they convince themselves that such things really exist."

No doubt some people who believe in God, and in the human spirit, do so merely as a result of "wishful thinking," Krystal, as you say. But I wonder if they really know what they are wishing for. The Bible says, "It is a terrible thing to fall into the hands of the living God"—terrible because He will not let you continue indefinitely a self-centered existence, focusing your life on your own pleasure and personal happiness. Rather, He will turn your life upside-down, if He has to, tipping you out of your bed of comfort to wake you up, so you can finally live in the light of Truth.

That's why the "wishful thinking" argument works the other way too. One could argue that those who do not believe in God, and in the human spirit, cling to their *disbelief* out of wishful thinking, because they would rather live shallow, self-centered, materialistic lives, and not have any supernatural Creator interfere with it. They certainly do not want to be answerable to an all-seeing God for their actions!

Clearly, these "wishful thinking" arguments cancel each other out; neither one is convincing on its own. Besides, we need to beware of philosophical arguments that are clearly *non-sequiturs*, for example, the claim that "no belief that gives us psychological comfort can possibly be true—it must be the product of wishful thinking." Why "must"? Couldn't it be the case that at least some of the truths we can discover about this world will be comforting and reassuring to us? Has our modern cynicism run so deep that we are no longer even open to the possibility?

Anyway, this is an example of one of the characteristic diseases of contemporary thought. The disease doesn't really have a name, as far as I know. C.S. Lewis called it "Bulverism" after someone he met. It essentially consists in this: *assuming someone is mistaken, and then attempting to explain how they went wrong before you have bothered to demonstrate that they are really mistaken in the first place*. For example, it may well be that a particular person with whom you are in dialogue is a victim of wishful thinking regarding the existence of God. But how do you know that is the case *before you* have examined their reasons for God's existence and found them to be fallacious? If their reasons for believing in God are really poor ones, then you can suggest that perhaps they went wrong because they let wishful thinking govern their opinions on the subject. But you can't automatically assume that in advance about every believer in God—unless you can clearly show that *all* of the arguments for the existence of God are fallacious. And that's a tall order.

Contemporary thought is rife with "Bulveristic" logic: "You only think that way because you are a male (or female);" "You only think that way because you are white (or black);" "You only think that way because you are middle class (or upper or lower class)." No doubt all of these factors— gender, race, and economic status—affect the way we think at times, to varying degrees. But it's not an argument against someone's point of view just to say, "You think that way merely because you are white/male/middle class etc."—that's a possible explanation of how someone went wrong, but first you have to fairly consider the actual reasons they give for their views, and deal with those. Only if you can show that those reasons are poor ones can you justly speculate about psychological explanations for their lapse into error.

In short, Krystal, beware of "Bulverism": it poisons rational discussion of just about any important topic these days. The "wishful thinking" argument is a perfect example of that.

> (3) "Anyway, you haven't really proven the existence of God, right? No one can. You have just shown that there are some arguments that point in favor, but there are some that point the other way, too (I think Marx and Freud and Nietszche offered famous ones). So in the end, isn't belief in God just a matter of faith?

To be honest, I am not much impressed by most of the arguments against the existence of God that I have heard, because almost all of them seem to be expressions of the "Nothing Buttery" that we discussed in our earlier letters, and as a result they fall victim to what philosophers call the trap of "Self-referential Absurdity." People fall into this trap when they make a claim about the whole world that can be shown to be self-contradictory when the claim is applied to the speaker himself. Logically, the speaker "saws off the branch on which he sits."

We met this already, Krystal, in our discussion of Reductionism a few months ago. Remember: the materialist holds that there is nothing but atoms and molecules bouncing around randomly in space—but that must include his own mind too, and if all of his thoughts are nothing but atoms and molecules bouncing around randomly in space, what reason do we have to take any of them seriously—including his reasons for believing that the whole universe is nothing but atoms and molecules? Logically speaking, he has shot himself in the foot!

Marxism falls into a similar trap. Karl Marx claimed that "all history is the history of class struggle," and therefore all the thoughts we think are determined by our place in our economic system. Religion itself is nothing but "the opiate of the masses," a kind of drug served up to the working class so they will keep dreaming of pie-in-the-sky-when-they-die rather than devote their energies to the struggle for equality and social justice. Well, if all our thoughts come from our position in the struggle between economic classes, then surely that applies to the thoughts of the Marxists themselves: they only think what they think because they are programmed by their place in the economic struggle to do so—so what reason do we have to take them seriously?

In fact, with Marxist logic one could fairly argue that Marxism itself is nothing more than "the opiate of upper-middle class university students," a kind of drug they take to ease their conscience because they find themselves among the "haves" who are getting ahead rather than among the "have-nots." Most of their families live materialistic lives, and are nominal churchgoers at best. Thus, as students they hope to ease their conscience about the plight of poor in a way that also fits within the materialistic, Nothing Buttery world in which they were bred. Trendy university Marxism fills their personal, psychological needs perfectly! So why should we take any of it seriously? On Marxism's own logic, Marxism itself is not based on objective, rational consideration of the facts.

James Sire in his book *The Universe Next Door* sums up the dilemma that all Marxist reductionism faces:

> Why should I work for a better society and try to end social exploitation? Marx rejects any moral values as a basis for such motivation. As a naturalist [nothing-buttery again!] he views morality simply as a product of human culture. There are no transcendent values which can be used as a basis for critically evaluating culture. Yet Marx himself often seems full of moral indignation as he looks at the excesses of capitalism. What is the basis for Marx's moral condemnation of capitalism if such moral notions as "justice" and "fairness" are just ideological inventions?[2]

Besides, Marxism has a host of other problems too, all of which were put on full display in the dark history of the 20th century. Sire sums it up pretty well:

> In theory, Marxism is supposed to benefit the working people and enable them to gain economic control of their own lives. In reality the bureaucratic rigidities of life under Communism [e.g. the bureaucratic centralization of power and a one-party state] led to economic stagnation as well as the loss of personal freedom.[3]

Then there are the followers of Sigmund Freud. For them, all human thinking and striving is driven by subconscious, irrational desires. Religion itself, with its alleged longings for the Infinite, its seemingly inconsolable desires (in this life) for the divine, is really nothing more than "wishful thinking"— a mere projection of the human need for complete security and erotic fulfillment. Indeed, all belief in God, and all human striving for meaning and purpose is seen as nothing but a projection of these inner drives for security, comfort, and sex.

Two things we can say here: First, if this were true, then the happiest people in the whole world should be those with the highest degree of security, comfort, and sexual pleasure in this life—but clearly, such is not the case. Modern western society is full to overflowing with people like this whose lives are tormented by depression, and whose families are torn by divorce, abortion, alcohol and drug abuse, and suicide. Even some of Freud's greatest followers in depth psychology, such as Victor Frankl and Carl Jung, abandoned Freud's Nothing Buttery perspective on religion and the pursuit of meaning. As Jung once said:

> Among all my patients in the second half of life—that is to say, over thirty-five—there is not one whose problem in the last resort was not that of finding a religious outlook on life. It is safe to say that every one of them fell ill because he had lost what the living religions of every age have given to their followers, and none of them has been really healed who did not regain his religious outlook.[4]

Second, if Freud has really found what lurks behind all human striving, then surely that applies to the efforts of the Freudians themselves: their own perspective, and their own strivings must be "nothing but" a projection of their own subconscious, irrational drives. So what "reason" do we have to take them seriously, if we know that they are not really driven by "reason" at all?

Finally, there is the philosopher Friedrich Nietzsche, whose books are more popular than ever these days. For Nietzsche all human thought and striving, including belief in God, is driven by the "will-to-power." There are really no rational belief systems at all, or rational social arrangements—all are nothing but masks for an endless power struggle. One wonders: doesn't that will-to-power include Nietzsche himself? On this reckoning, his own philosophical arguments must be nothing but an expression of his personal will-to-power (for recognition, fame, and influence perhaps) so why should we treat his philosophy as any more defensible, or convincing, than any other philosophy? Nietzsche has effectively sawed off the branch on which he was sitting: Self-referential Absurdity strikes again!

Marx, Freud, Nietzsche—they all found fragments of truth, of course. Human life is indeed sometimes driven by economic forces, inner drives for security and sex, and by a "will-to-power." But it cannot be true that all human thought and striving are reducible to "nothing but" these things—not without falling into the trap of Self-referential Absurdity. One who believes in the existence of God can take a broader, more liberal view. We can accept that people often succumb to these irrational influences, allowing them to govern their lives, and yet we know that there is far more to the human story than that.

Last of all, Krystal, you suggested that no one can prove the existence of God anyway, and so belief in God must ultimately be an act of faith, rather than rational certainty.

I think that all depends upon what you mean by "prove."

Perhaps philosophers cannot "prove" that God exists in quite the same way that we can prove something in mathematics. For example, proving that two plus two equals four gives you absolute, mathematical certainty. But there is another kind of "proof" which justifies another kind of certainty. Philosophers traditionally call this "moral certainty." We reach it when we have a number of arguments and evidences that converge, that all point in the same direction. Put together enough of these converging arguments and you can come to a conclusion that something is "true beyond a reasonable doubt."

That is how a court of law works. A jury does not convict someone of a crime based on absolute, mathematical certainty of his guilt—which would be impossible to attain anyway—but on the basis of the overwhelming strength of the converging evidence. The fingerprints on the gun, a motive, an opportunity, a faked alibi—none of these things on their own would convince a jury to convict a man, but put them all together and they all point in the same direction: a cumulative case for a guilty verdict "beyond a reasonable doubt."

Moral certainty, at least, is what Philosophy can offer us about God, I think. Over the last few months, Krystal, I have shared with you several philosophical pathways to the existence of God. Perhaps no single one of them, on its own, would be entirely convincing, but put them together and you have converging arguments that all point to the same Reality.

Think back to our previous letters. Our longing for something that nothing on this earth can ever satisfy, we said, is most likely a longing for a God who really exists: the perfect, boundless Good. Then we saw that it is more likely that the intricate, stable, and pervasive order that we find in nature is the product of a supernatural Intelligent Designer than the product of mere chance. And later we said that the best explanation for the inner Light of conscience that beckons us all to do good and avoid evil, and puts an absolute claim upon us, is that it was placed in us by an Absolute Being.

Perhaps you have noticed that each of these pathways to God also points to the others. For example, if it is likely that a God who is "perfect, boundless Good" really exists, then among His boundless perfections would be infinite Power and infinite Wisdom, in other words, a boundless capacity for intelligent design. If an Intelligent Designer of the universe really exists, then it is likely that He would have designed free and rational creatures like us with an inner compass, an inner Light, to help us live in harmony with His design, to discern right from wrong. And the God whose character is manifested in that inner Light is evidently one who is totally committed to Good.

In short, since all of these mysteries point in the same direction, we can be sure of His existence "beyond a reasonable doubt."

It certainly takes faith to live out that truth, Krystal: to put your complete trust in Him, to let Him be your inner Strength, and guiding Light. But it doesn't take faith just to know that He is there.

He gave each one of us the light of reason, and the light of reason leads us back to Him.

Love always,

Uncle Robert

9. Physics and the Self-Creating Universe

Hi Krystal,

It must feel good to be "heading down the home stretch," so to speak, with only your final exams left to finish of your first year at university. If it's any consolation, you're having a better start in College than I did: I failed ancient Greek in my first spring semester, ruining my hopes to be a Classics major, and had to withdraw from school for a year because I was so depressed—about that, and many other things. Not a happy time!

I understand, however, that you are having your struggles too—not least with the subjects we have been discussing by e-mail over the past few months. I am glad that you found helpful what I shared with you last time, but I understand why you say that you are "still not entirely sure" about the existence of God. For me, the existence of God can be rationally demonstrated "beyond a reasonable doubt," but you politely replied, "The trouble is, you have not addressed all my doubts!"

From your last letter, it appears that your Physics professor succeeded in sowing some new ones. You said that in the last class of the semester, he tried to show that "Physics has done away with the need for God to account for the existence of the universe." Drawing upon the new book *The Grand Design* by Stephen Hawking and Leonard Mlodinow, he argued that we can now explain the existence of our universe by a "quantum fluctuation," the "dynamical laws" of which are presently being worked out by the experts. In short, natural laws are responsible for bringing the universe into existence out of nothing—hence, the most famous quote from the book:

Because there is a law such as gravity, the universe can and will create itself from nothing. Spontaneous creation is the reason there is something rather than nothing, why the universe exists, why we exist. It is not necessary to invoke God to light the blue touch paper and set the universe going.[1]

All this is not surprising to me: atheism is trendy at North American universities these days, so why shouldn't you find it in Physics class too? What worries me more, however, is the same thing that got you miffed: in the midst of explaining Hawking's theory, and passing out excerpts from Hawking's book to read, your prof never discussed the writings of anyone who believes in the existence of a Creator-God, and critiques the "Quantum Fluctuation" idea as an explanation for the existence of the universe or multiverse. In fact, when you raised your hand and asked him about it, your prof did not seem to be aware of these critiques at all, except to dismiss them with scorn as "just the complaints of theologians." But there are plenty of leading scientists and philosophers who believe in God, and have addressed these matters in depth. Sadly, your Physics prof has just "buried his head in the sand" on this one.

You asked me whether I could set you on to any good articles or book chapters to "let the other side be heard." Yes, I can. In this letter I will share with you two of my favorites.

Just to be sure we are on the same page here, as I understand it, the "Quantum Fluctuation Theory" basically states that universes might come into being through the same physical process by which subatomic particles in a vacuum seem to appear out of nowhere in our universe.

There are several variants of this theory—Hawking's is only one of them—but the best response I have read to his book was by Stephen M. Barr, who is a professor of Physics at the University of Delaware, and author of *Modern Physics and Ancient Faith*. It's called "Much Ado About Nothing: Stephen Hawking and the Self-Creating Universe." I'll quote his online article at length for you, but be sure to read the whole thing when you get the chance. Barr writes:

> Right up front, it must be noted that [Hawking's] idea is extremely speculative, has not yet been formulated in a mathematically rigorous way, and is unable at this point to make testable predictions. Indeed, it is very hard to imagine how it could ever be tested. It would be more accurate to call these "scenarios" rather than theories....

> [The basic idea is that] when the number of universes changes [in a system of universes, also known as a multiverse], it is because that single overarching system has undergone a transition from one of its "quantum states" to another. Such transitions are precisely governed by dynamical laws (assumed to include the laws of quantum mechanics). These laws would govern not only how many universes there were, but the characteristics of these universes, such as how many dimensions of space they could have and what kinds of matter and forces they could contain....

> The dramatic possibility Hawking is considering (and many others before him) is that such a system might make a transition from [a] "no-universe state" to a state with one or more universes....

> Would it be creation *ex nihilo*, creation from nothing?

> The answer is no. First of all, one is not starting from "nothing." The "no-universe" state in these speculative scenarios is not nothing, it is a very definite something: it is one particular quantum state among many of an intricate rule-governed system. The no-universe state has specific properties and potentialities defined by a system of mathematical laws.

An analogy may help here. A checking account is a system that has many possible states.... Even if your checking account happens to be in the zero-dollar state one day, the checking account is nevertheless still something definite and real—not "nothing." It presupposes a bank, a monetary system, a contract between you and that bank—all being governed by various systems of rules.

Imagine the day on which your bank account is zero. Then imagine a deposit the next day that raises it to one thousand dollars. A quantum theory of the creation of the universe (in Hawking's version, or Vilenkin's, or anyone else's) is akin to this transition from an empty account to one full of money.... The "no-universe" of [Hawking's] speculations is like the "no-dollars" in my account. It exists within the framework of a complex overarching system with specific rules. So we can see that, if true, the way of thinking put forward by Hawking does not threaten the classical doctrine of creation [of the universe by God] out of nothing [In other words, at most Hawking's scenario merely describes how a universe or multiverse system might possibly bring another universe into being—although he has no scientific proof of this claim, of course]....

Non-scientists are quick to ask the obvious questions. Why a system obeying quantum mechanics, M-theory, superstring theory, or whatever laws of physics that make scientific speculations possible in the first place? Why not no system at all, with no laws at all, no anything, just blank non-being?[2]

In fact, Hawking—and your Physics professor—have fallen victim to what we would call in Philosophy a "category error." "Dynamical Laws" alone cannot answer the question of why there is a universe or multiverse, because "laws" all by themselves cannot cause anything to be or to happen. Natural "laws" are merely *descriptive* statements: abstract numerical statements that tell you how the particles and forces in a system or universe are likely to behave *if you already have one in existence.*

"Abstract" equations cannot cause anything to happen or to be in the real world, because by definition they are not "concrete": they are "virtual" rather than "actual" existing things. In other words, they only exist in the mind, and can only *describe* what exists or what possibly might exist—but they cannot actually do anything on their own in the real world. Only a real person who has such abstractions in his mind can actually do or cause anything with them. Now, if there is an all-knowing, all-powerful God, and He had such laws in mind….

Anyway, to go back to Barr's bank account analogy: the rules of the bank cannot deposit any money into your empty checking account. Just an abstract set of bank rules could never cause anything to exist or happen at all. First you need some real concrete money somewhere to which those rules can apply, and then someone to cause that money to obey those rules. So where does the money come from in the first place—and what causes the money to obey those rules, rather than some other set, or none at all? Barr concludes:

> Physics, by its very nature, cannot answer these questions. And the funny thing is that Hawking himself is perfectly aware of this. Indeed, he said it himself in a previous book! In *A Brief History of Time*, Hawking observed—quite correctly— that any theory of physics is "just a set of rules and equations." And he asked, "What is it that breathes fire into the equations and makes a universe for them to describe? The usual approach of science of constructing a mathematical model cannot answer the question of why there should be a universe for the model to describe."…

> As Hawking once understood, equations may turn out to be accurate descriptions of some reality, but cannot *confer* reality on the things they describe.[3]

I like Dinesh D'Souza's summary of the point best of all:

> It takes more than laws to make a universe. If you have a blueprint for a car, that doesn't by itself produce a car. As Hawking concedes, we still don't know what or who put the fire into the equations.[4]

The second article I want to share with you, Krystal, can also be found on the internet, but this one is written by a friend of mine, Michael Horner, entitled *"Does God Exist?"* Horner effectively "turns the tables" on Hawking and co. by showing that if we take a multi-disciplinary approach—utilizing philosophy, science, and mathematics together—we can make a strong case that a Creator-God is the best explanation for the beginning of the universe.

Again, I will quote his essay to you at length, but be sure to track down and read the whole thing.[5] He summarizes the approach of many philosophers and scientists who are convinced "theists" (believers in the existence of God), relying especially upon the work of philosopher William Lane Craig.

Horner starts with a clear outline of his argument:

> Premise 1) Whatever begins to exist must have a cause.
> Premise 2) The universe began to exist
> Premise 3) Therefore the universe has a cause

In defense of the first premise, Horner states that most of us have no problem accepting this belief; in other words, it is a self-evident statement (a "properly basic belief," if you remember my very first letter to you, Krystal!). Anyway, it's called the "Principle of Causation:" that there is a sufficient reason, a sufficient cause, for everything that comes into being or happens. We assume its truth in virtually every aspect of our daily lives, and our daily experience constantly confirms it and never denies it. If a fire is raging, something (lightening, a match) must have caused it; if the rain is pelting down, some confluence of environmental factors are responsible for it. It's a foundational premise both of science and philosophy. It's also one reason why a child pesters its parents with the question "why?"—and never would be satisfied with the response, "oh, there's no reason why."

Some people today argue that this is precisely what we see happening at a sub-atomic level: particles seem to pop into being suddenly, out of nowhere, without a cause. However, this is a misunderstanding of the scientific evidence. Particles do not come into being out of nothing. As Philosopher William Lane Craig explains:

> They arise as spontaneous fluctuations of the energy contained in the sub-atomic vacuum, which constitutes an indeterministic cause of their origin…. Popular magazine articles touting such theories as getting "something from nothing" simply do not understand that the vacuum is not nothing, but a sea of fluctuating energy endowed with a rich structure and subject to physical laws.[6]

Besides, the mere fact that particles appear suddenly in our visual or instrumental field would not entitle us to conclude that they originated out of nothing (*ex nihilo*), and without any cause at all. After all, the particles could have re-appeared from somewhere else, or something or someone invisible could have caused them to pop into existence at that moment. Even Stephen Hawking assumes that some factor—natural "laws"—must be the answer to the question of why any universe came into existence at all. The answer can't be "there is no answer, no reason, nothing caused it to pop into being one day." After all "nothing" is the very opposite of something, and by the basic law of logic, The Law of Non-Contradiction (remember again my first letter to you!) nothing can't behave like something! For the very definition of "nothing" is that it is a sheer void that cannot cause things to be or to happen. If a universe comes into being, therefore, it must have a real cause, a really existing "something" behind it.

By the way, that is also why phrases such as "spontaneous creation" and "self-creating universe" really make no sense at all. They are self-contradictory. There can be no such thing as a "self-creating" universe, or a "self-creating" anything else for that matter. Nothing can create itself, for a thing has to exist already in order to be able to do anything like create, "spontaneously" or otherwise.

In defense of his second premise, Horner, as I said, takes a multi-disciplinary approach:

> We have both scientific confirmation and logical argument for the universe having a beginning. According to the standard Big Bang model, space, time, matter, and energy all came into existence simultaneously around 15 billion years ago.
>
> Furthermore, according to the Second Law of Thermodynamics, given enough time the universe will eventually reach a state of equilibrium—a cold, dark, dead, virtually motionless state. Clearly, if the universe is without a beginning, then there has been an infinite length of time preceding this present moment. If this is the case, then the universe should already be in a state of equilibrium. This should be a cold, dark, dead, virtually motionless universe. There should be no galaxies, solar systems, stars or planets— not to mention living organisms. Since there is obviously plenty of heat, light, movement, and life, the past must not be finite. The universe had a beginning.

Horner's final point, in defense of his second premise, shows that not only our universe, but any conceivable universe or multiverse must have a beginning:

> The third and strongest piece of support for the beginning of the universe comes from the impossibility of an infinite past.

This is because *an actual infinite number of anything cannot exist in the real world.*

We might think that since we use the concept of infinity in mathematics there would be no problem here. But mathematicians who work with the concept of infinity do so by adopting some arbitrary rules to avoid the absurdities and contradictions that come with an infinite number of anything. And these rules don't apply to the real world. Infinity only works in the abstract realm, and only with some special rules.

To see the absurdity and contradictions of an actual infinite number of things in the real world, imagine a library having an infinite number of black books and an infinite number of green books alternating colors on the shelves and numbered consecutively on the spines.

Does it make any sense to say that there are as many black books as there are black plus green books together? Not really, but that is what you would have to say if you want to claim the infinite is possible in the real world.

Suppose we withdrew all the green books. How many books are there left in the library? There would still be an infinite number of books in the library even though we just withdrew an infinite number and found a way to get them home! Suppose we withdrew the books numbered 4, 5, 6,… and so on. Now how many books are left? Three! Something is surely wrong here. One time we subtract an infinite number of books and we're left with an infinite number; the next time we subtract an infinite number and we're left with three—a clear logical contradiction. Since our hypothesis leads to a contradiction, the hypothesis must be false: a library with an infinite number of books cannot exist….

Therefore, since a beginningless past [also] would be an actual infinite number of things (events) and since an infinite number of things cannot exist in the real world, *it follows logically that the past is not infinite. The universe [or multiverse, if there is one] had a beginning.*

Furthermore, an infinite past is impossible, because an actual infinite cannot be formed by adding one member after another. It's like counting to infinity—you just never get there. Just like we can never finish counting to infinity, we can never begin to count down from a negative infinity. But to have a universe with no beginning, you would have to have an infinite number of past events leading up to the present. But this is impossible, because by implication, the present could never have come to exist.

Thus the Big Bang Theory, the Second Law of Thermodynamics and the impossibility of an infinite past all support the universe having a beginning.

Since whatever begins to exist must have a cause, it follows logically that the universe has a cause.

Horner finishes by asking what sort of universal "cause" this must be. Clearly, it must be a cause that is not bound by space, time, matter, and energy, since it brought all of these things into being. And it must be a cause powerful enough and intelligent enough to bring all things into being. So what have we got: an all-powerful, all-knowing, eternal (not bounded by time) "Spirit" (not bounded by space, matter and energy). Hmmm…sounds suspiciously like "God," don't you think?

And if someone asks: "Then who made God? What caused God to exist?" the answer should be clear—"God is the one being who does not need to have a cause." Remember that Horner's first premise was the self-evident Principle of Causation: "whatever *begins to exist* must have a cause." But according to Horner's argument, God stands outside of time—in fact, He brought space, time, matter and energy of the universe or multiverse into existence in the first place. If He stands outside of time, then He did not "begin to exist" at some point. Rather, He *always* existed. He is eternal. Therefore, He does not need to be made or caused-to-exist. He simply is.

However, even this argument for God, is not (to my mind at least) the strongest one of all. For it is partially based on scientific theories (the standard Big Bang model, and the Second Law of Thermodynamics) and scientific theories can change, and sometimes do. But there is another way to answer the great question of all philosophical questions, Krystal; I mean:

"Why is there something rather than nothing?"

I didn't write to you about this yet one because I knew that in order to understand it properly, you would need to learn the meaning of a bunch of philosophical terms, such as "contingency," "essence," "substance," "accident," and "the Principle of Sufficient Reason." However, since you have been troubled by your Physics profs' (and Stephen Hawking's) attempts to find a God-less reason for the existence of the universe, I will set aside some time to write to you again, and share with you the answer of some of the greatest philosophers of all time, such as Thomas Aquinas and Gottfried Leibniz, and why they believed that reason can show us that there is a Creator after all.

I know you are still struggling with these things, Krystal, and that your heart and mind still may not be at rest about this God-business. Remember that if there really is a God who made you, and this whole universe, then He is not just *something to think about*, like thinking about a rock or a tree or a distant galaxy; rather, He is *Someone* you can actually have some kind of relationship with. As you are *nearly* convinced that He exists, why not reach out to Him in prayer and ask Him to make it clear to you that He does? I mean, what have you got to lose? If He doesn't exist, then it will become clear in time that you have just been talking to the wall. Big deal! I talk to the wall all the time when I am mumbling and grumbling about life's petty frustrations!

What I am trying to say is that our God-given reason is a springboard to a relationship (I think that's one of the reasons why He gave it to us in the first place). But a springboard doesn't get you anywhere unless you jump on it. I think you are ready to jump, and see what happens.

Meanwhile, my prayer for you is really no different than my constant prayer for myself. I turn to it often, especially when I am weary, tired out from life's trials and disappointments. I stole it from one of my favorite philosophers of all, the ancient philosopher Boethius:

> Grant, Father, that our minds Thy august seat may scan,
> Grant us the sight of true good's source, and grant us light
> That we may fix on Thee our mind's unblinded eye.
> Disperse the clouds of earthly matter's cloying weight;
> Shine out in all Thy glory; for Thou art rest and peace
> To those who worship Thee; to see Thee is our end,
> Who art our source and maker, lord and path and goal.[7]

Love,

Uncle Robert

10. The Wonder of Existence

Dear Krystal,

Congratulations on the successful completion of your first year at university! Your mom told me you did very well on your final exams, and that you are now "chilling out" for a while at home. I had hoped to pay you all a visit this week, but there are still some things I need to take care of before my own academic year is complete. I'll try to catch up with you before you leave for your summer job at the park.

Meanwhile, with all the marking of essays and exams done for the year, I have some extra time on my hands in the evenings, and so I wanted to keep my promise to you from my last letter. I promised to share with you what I think is the strongest argument of all for the existence of God. The picture is just not complete without it. After all, we can speak of God as the likely source of the universal human longing for perfect, boundless Good. We can speak of Him as the most likely author of order and design in the universe, and as most the likely source of the Natural Moral law, shining in every human heart. We can even say that if (as seems likely) the universe or multiverse had a beginning in time, then there must be a transcendent, eternal, all-knowing, all-powerful Cause of its existence. All of this rolled together makes what we could call a strong "cumulative case" for God's existence. That is certainly what I was trying to argue in my last few letters to you.

Still, the ultimate philosophical question is not, "How can we best account for this or that feature of human experience, or of the universe?" but, "Why is there something, rather than nothing at all?"

It's not an "ivory tower" question. It's not a question dreamed up by intellectuals somewhere. Rather, it is a question born of the childlike wonder in us all. It's what strikes every one of us on days when we wake up in the morning and look out on the world and realize: *"None of this has to be here!* It would violate no law of logic if everything we see had never existed in the first place, or if it all vanished five minutes from now. So why is it all here? Why does anything exist at all?"

In fact, the answer to this question is easy enough to understand. The common man on the street knows very well that there must be a reason, an explanation for the whole show. And the only sufficient reason for everything that exists is God.

I promised to you that I would draw upon insights from two of the greatest philosophers of all time, Thomas Aquinas and Gottfried Leibniz, and show you how they spelled out this argument. But I know that once I get started, Krystal—given your love for literature and your artistic temperament—you are bound to think: "This is all so dry and pedantic! Can this really be the pathway to discovering the reality of God?" Well, it's not the pathway, of course; it's only one of many. But in terms of what human reason can do, it's a very clear and powerful one. Just remember that in the biblical story, the way to the Promised Land passes through the clear skies and barren sands of the desert! So this path may seem as dry as dust at first, but the final destination is well worth the trouble.

OK, let the journey through the desert begin!

1. **Every existing thing** (in other words, every "being," "entity," or "substance"—these words can be used interchangeably) **must either depend for its existence upon other things** (in which case, it is called a "contingent being") or solely upon itself (in which case it is called a "self-existent" being). Logically, those seem to be the only two options: contingency or self-existence.

Take a moment to familiarize yourself with these terms, Krystal, because we will need them for the rest of the dusty trail!

2. **We observe many contingent beings in the universe**. For example, the plants and animals depend upon the warmth of the sun, the refreshment of water, and the anchor of planetary gravity in order to exist. The Milky Way Galaxy depends upon the energy given to its stars by the Big Bang, and the forces of gravitation to exist—and so on. In short, contingent beings are beings that depend upon "causes" for their existence, and we never seem to meet a being in our experience that does not.

3. **Can every existing thing be contingent?** If the answer is "yes," then there would be no sufficient reason for the existence of any contingent being within the universe. For if we questioned any entity in such a universe as to why it exists, it would respond: "Don't look to me for the sufficient reason why I exist; after all, I am merely a 'contingent' being; I depend for my existence on other things—so go ask them!" And then when we asked the question of those things, they would say the same thing to us—and so on and on, forever. The result would be an infinite regress of reasons for the existence of things (i.e., an endless string of causes of existence); so the question of why any entity in the world exists would never be sufficiently or finally answered, only endlessly asked!

4. **The only sufficient reason for the existence of contingent things in this universe, therefore, must be a self-existent being, one who does not depend at all upon any other being for His existence, and who can bestow existence on other things. That self-existent Source of all existence is what we commonly refer to as God.**

Well, Krystal, it's clear that this argument depends upon the principle that there must be a "sufficient reason" for everything. We discussed a more limited version of this principle in our last set of letters to each other, the Principle of Causation: that everything that comes into being or happens has a cause. The Principle of Sufficient Reason, however, is even broader than that, because it states that there must be a sufficient explanation for the existence and actions of everything, whether it comes into being or starts to happen one day or not. The existence even of eternal, everlasting things, therefore, must be explained or accounted for somehow. This argument says that to account for the existence of anything there are only two options: "contingency" and "self-existence." Everything that exists cannot be contingent (or the Principle of Sufficient Reason would be violated); therefore there must be a self-existent, ultimate Source of all being. His name is God.

I hope you can see that this argument for the existence of God is not really very complicated, despite the fancy terminology. Things get a bit "stickier," however, when we consider the main objections that have been raised to this philosophical argument over the past few centuries.

a. **We have no reason to believe that the Principle of Sufficient Reason (PSR) universally applies**. In other words, why must everything have a sufficient reason for its existence or its actions?

It seems to me, Krystal, that with the PSR we are once again dealing with a "properly basic" or "self-evident" belief. We always assume that our "why" questions must have a sufficient answer, if only we were smart enough and could see enough to find all the answers. That is why, from earliest childhood we endlessly ask the question, "why?" in every field of knowledge and endeavor. Going back to the very first letter

I sent to you, Krystal, we can say that the PSR fulfills Thomas Reid's criteria for a "properly basic belief'—and that puts the burden of proof strongly on those who contest it, not on those who uphold it.

In fact, this puts the detractors of the PSR in a difficult spot: for the only way rational people are going to be convinced that the PSR does not universally apply is if someone can give us a "sufficient reason" for any alleged limitation of it!

In any case, no one has ever offered any good reason why the PSR would apply in one area of reality and human inquiry rather than another. The fact that we face special obstacles in finding sufficient reasons for things in some areas, such as quantum physics and philosophical metaphysics, is no reason to doubt the universal validity of the PSR itself. These obstacles can be explained by a variety of factors. First, there are limitations on our human capacity for empirical observation (that is, we can only observe so much of the world with our five senses— e.g., we cannot see an electron with our eyes, only the effects caused by electrons on our scientific instruments). Second, there is the complexity of the natural order—which in some respects may just be too subtle for our finite minds to figure out. Third, there is the necessity for us to use analogical language when speaking of the immaterial realm of being (in other words, to talk about God and the soul we can only say what these realities are "like" from our human experience, because we cannot observe them directly—so God is in some ways "like" an endless ocean, or the soul is "like" a breath of wind). We have to use analogical language when talking about non-observable entities in the physical realm as well, such as sub-atomic realities: so electrons are not really little spherical planets circling around atomic nuclei, but they are somewhat like that (which is why your high school science teacher showed you models of atoms based on such analogies).

None of this implies that there are no sufficient reasons for the existence and actions of sub-atomic or immaterial beings. The limitations of the human vantage point on reality cannot be allowed to dictate what really exists. Thus, the "burden of proof" has not been met by the detractors of the PSR. For any rational person the Principle must stand.

b. **Perhaps there are no necessary cause-and-effect relationships at all in the universe—or at least none that we can be sure about.** In other words, maybe we only think that all events have sufficient causes because our minds "project" this pattern onto the reality we experience. Or maybe we make an unwarranted assumption that events that constantly happen in sequence are actually the result of "causation." What reason do we really have to believe in the Principle of Causation anyway: that everything that comes into being or happens must have a sufficient cause?

In a nutshell, these are some of the classical objections by 18th century philosophers Immanuel Kant and David Hume to all rational arguments for a "First Cause" of the universe.

Hume rejected the idea of necessary cause-and-effect relationships in the world on the grounds that all that we really perceive in our experience are constant conjunctions of events. In other words, we experience objects in constant spatial and temporal conjunction with each other, so that events of one kind regularly just happen to be followed by events of another kind. For example, whenever we put fire under a pot of water, the water begins to boil. We notice such constant conjunctions and so our minds form habits of associating one kind of event with another kind of event. Past experience habitually tells us what to expect. But in reality, we have no real reason to believe that one event (applying heat) actually "causes" the other to happen (water to boil), or that it must always happen that way in the future. The one kind of event always just happens to follow the other in our experience—and that's all that reason can tell us with any certainty. Needless to say, if we cannot be sure on rational grounds of the apparent cause and effect patterns in nature that we experience every day, we can hardly be sure that the whole universe must consists of a chain of causes and effects reaching right back to an ultimate First Cause. So, down in flames goes my argument for God as the First Cause of all Creation!

Well, not so fast.

To begin to answer Hume we can go right back to what we discussed earlier, Krystal. The Principle of Causation, like the broader Principle of Sufficient Reason, has all the hallmarks of a "properly basic belief." Remember my first letter to you? There I said that we do not need to have a reason for such beliefs, because they are really at the foundation of all rational thought. The burden of proof, therefore, surely rests on the detractors of such properly basic beliefs, to show why they do not apply to the real world in which we live.

Has Hume shown that? I hardly think so.

For one thing, Hume's analysis of human psychology is faulty. The human mind is surely able to distinguish between constant conjunctions of events and actual cause and effect relationships between events. For example, from the beginning of the human race, people have observed night following day with unbroken regularity. But I do not know of any culture—or indeed, of anyone at all—who ever felt forced to conclude by this regular sequence of events that day actually causes night to happen!

Second, if Hume has succeeded in undermining "First Cause" arguments for the existence of God, he has only done so at a terrible cost: for the whole edifice of modern science also collapses under Hume's wrecking ball! After all, scientists purport to give us an account of how nature actually works: the causes for natural events within the natural order. But Hume claims that this kind of knowledge is impossible; all that we actually perceive are constant conjunctions of events. Historian of philosophy T.Z. Lavine sums it up in her book *From Socrates to Sartre: The Philosophic Quest*:

> Not only is metaphysics impossible, science is also impossible. The causal laws of science have been reduced by Hume to the psychological laws of the association of ideas. There is no necessary connection between causes and effects…. Science cannot provide objective causal explanations of events or predict the future, since there is no justification for the assumption that the regularities observed in the past will continue in the future.[1]

In short, Krystal, people can take-on-board Hume's skepticism if they wish, but only at the cost of denying that modern science gives us any real, objective knowledge about the natural world in which we live.

Immanuel Kant's perspective is a bit more difficult to describe, and there wouldn't be space for me to go into all the nuances of it here. Suffice it to say that Kant held that our minds organize and unify the flux of reality that we experience with the help of twelve pure rational concepts (in other words, concepts that come from within the human mind itself). That is the only way we can begin to make sense of the variety of experiences and impressions that we receive from the world around us. These purely subjective concepts include "forms of intuition" such as space and time, and "categories" such as cause and substance. As historian of Philosophy George F. Thomas explained:

> Our sense impressions are ordered in relation to one another in space and they occur in succession to one another in time. But they are ordered in these ways, not because space and time are objective realities in which objects are located and events occur, but because they are subjective forms which we bring with us to all our sense experience and by means of

which we relate our impressions to one another.... Similarly,
[the mind] possesses categories such as substance and cause
by means of which it relates the "manifold" of sense
impressions to one another and organizes them into a
coherent whole of objects of experience.[2]

Finally, these forms and categories that all come from
within our own minds, when combined with our sensory
experience of the world, give rise within us to "synthetic *a
priori* judgments" such as "every event must have a cause"—
the Principle of Causation.

Pretty complex stuff! But it's not hard to see where all this
leads us in the end: once again, modern scientific knowledge is
rendered suspect. As Lavine tells us, according to Kant:

Nature does not give the human mind its laws—it is the other
way around. The mind gives its own laws to nature—its own
laws in the form of necessary concepts which organize all
sensory materials.... In Kant's famous words, "mind is the
law-giver to nature." Thus the laws of nature are dependent
upon the concepts of the human mind.[3]

Well Krystal, if that is how the human mind actually
works—and Kant does not actually *prove* this, he merely
outlines it as a theory—then it is easy to see how it
overthrows any idea that we can deduce the existence of a
First Cause of the universe—for the Principle of Causation
itself is really only a partial product of our own minds. The
trouble is this also seems to undermine the claim that science
can give us real, objective knowledge of the actual world in
which we live. Kant himself says that we can never know what
things really are in themselves (noumena) only how they
appear to us (phenomena).

But this raises an even bigger question, for if our
knowledge of the real world (noumena) is so heavily shaped
and colored by our own subjective concepts, with even

"space," "time," "cause" and "substance" as projections upon reality from our own minds, then how do we really know that there is any world beyond our own minds to begin with? The arguments Kant gave in response to this question were not very convincing. That is one reason why, in the 19th century, many philosophers wandered down the blind alleys of philosophical idealism (Hegel) and radical subjectivism (Kierkegaard): because the capacity of human reason to know anything outside of our own minds had been so completely undermined by Kant.

Quite apart from the philosophical merits and demerits of the views of Kant and Hume on these matters, Krystal, I remain perpetually astonished at all such *counter-intuitive mental gymnastics*, where the "properly basic" is largely thrown out the window. Much of this, it would seem, was just to avoid having to accept the rational deduction of a single Source and Giver of all existence. Kind'a makes you wonder, doesn't it…?

c. **Perhaps the universe or multiverse as a whole could be the sufficient reason for its own existence**. In other words, why do we have to reach beyond the universe in order to find a self-existent being, a God, to account for everything that exists? Individual things in this world may come into being and pass away—we know from Physics that individual particles within the universe are generated and annihilated every day—but the universe itself may be the self-existent source of it all.

There are several problems with this line of reasoning, I think.

First of all, if the natural universe of space-time-matter-energy (or multiverse, if there is one) was really the self-existent, ultimate reason for the existence of everything in it, then, clearly, that universe would never have had a beginning: it always would have existed, and always will. But remember my last letter: it seems that one can make a strong case from modern science (the Big Bang, and the Second Law of Thermodynamics), that our universe had a beginning. As we also saw, from a consideration of the impossibility of the existence of an infinite number of items or events in the real world, any conceivable universe or multiverse must have had a beginning. At the moment of that beginning, it could not bring itself into being out of nothing (because—remember from last time—"nothing" cannot produce "something"); so why does it exist now? In short, the universe or multiverse cannot be the sufficient reason for its own existence.

Second, if we take a closer look at what a "self-existent being" means, we will see that a changing universe cannot be such a being anyway.

"Existence" is, after all, a funny word. As the philosopher Immanuel Kant pointed out, it cannot be a natural attribute of a thing; I mean, if you describe your boyfriend, Krystal, you would never say he is "tall, dark, handsome, intelligent, kind—and existing." Existence is not an attribute of a thing, alongside others; it is what any entity has to have in order to have any real attributes at all. In other words, Krystal, existence is not a particular natural attribute of boyfriends or of your boyfriend; it's just what your boyfriend has got to have that insures he is not a mere figment of your imagination!

So the universe, if it is self-existent, cannot just have as one of its natural attributes the power to exist; it must have existence already in order to have any natural attributes at all.

Then, perhaps, "existence" is not a particular attribute alongside others of a self-existent thing, but the entire definition or "essence" of it. In other words, *a self-existent being could be defined as the very power and fullness of all that it can possibly mean "to be."* If the universe was a self-existent being, therefore, it would be Being itself, the ultimate Being—and Being itself surely needs no explanation beyond itself.

However, if that is what it means to be "self-existent" (and what else could it possibly mean?), then the universe as we know it cannot be a self-existent being. For Being itself, the power and fullness of all that it can possibly mean "to be," can have no un-actualized potentials in it. What I mean is, at every moment, it must be fulfilling all the potentials of Being, enacting all that Being can be. Otherwise, it would not be Being itself, but some partial, incomplete form of being striving to fulfill its potentials over time. There can be no alternative or temporary ways for Being itself to exist other than as the complete fullness of Being, so it could have no changing states. But there is change going on all the time in our universe and in any conceivable multiverse; therefore the universe or multiverse cannot be a self-existent being; it cannot be the sufficient reason for its own existence.

The sufficient reason for the existence of the universe, therefore, must transcend all ever-changing universes. That's one reason we call Him God.

d. **Perhaps we have committed the so-called "fallacy of composition"?** In other words, just because something is true of all the members of a group, it does not necessarily follow that it is true of the group as a whole. For example, every tennis ball in a group of tennis balls may be round, but that does not necessarily mean that the group as a whole is round (the balls might be arranged on a tennis court in a triangle shape). So, just because the universe may be full of nothing but contingent beings, it does not necessarily follow that the universe as a whole must be contingent, dependent upon some external, self-existent source for its being.

Here, Krystal, we need to bear in mind that *sometimes* what is true of the parts of a whole or the members of a group is indeed true of the whole group. For example, if every brick in a wall is red, the brick wall as a whole (unless someone has painted it otherwise) will be red.

So what kind of "group" do we have if we are talking about the group of "all contingent beings"?

In order to answer this, Krystal, we have to make another distinction: a distinction (drawn from classical Philosophy) between what is "accidental" and what is "essential" to a substance. The "accidental" features of a substance or entity are modifications of it, modifications in quantity, quality, and relationship. For example, a beautiful woman might lose most of her quantity of hair from a wasting disease, and no longer be physically beautiful, but she is still "essentially" a human being. In a similar way, "red" is an "accidental" quality of a brick (you can have different colored bricks, such as brown and yellow bricks). But "roundness" is of the very "essence" of a tennis ball—all "balls" by definition are round or oval. If it's not round or oval shaped, it cannot be a "ball."

Consider: a whole group of bricks, each one with the "accidental" quality of "redness" would of necessity be red, but a whole group of tennis balls, each one with the "essential" attribute of "roundness" would not necessarily be round. So it appears that a group as a whole will manifest the "accidental" properties common to every member of the group, but not necessarily the "essential" properties common to each member.

Now, "contingency" would be an accidental, not an essential property of any substance. Clearly, "contingency" has to do with the relationship between a substance and other substances (a relationship of dependency). Thus, a universe consisting only of contingent beings would itself be a contingent universe, just as a wall consisting of nothing but red bricks would be red. And a universe with nothing but contingent beings cannot explain its own existence: it has to have a Creator.

e. **Perhaps there is more than one self-existent being?** In other words, why couldn't there be more than one self-existent being as the sufficient reason for the existence of everything? Doesn't your argument lead us just as easily to believe in many gods as to believe in one?

Well, for one thing, we have no reason to believe that there is more than one self-existent being as the sufficient reason for the existence of the universe or multiverse *because only one is sufficient!* We just don't need to posit the existence of any more than one to explain what needs explaining. One self-existent being, who is Being itself (that is, with the power and fullness of "existence" as His own "essence") is all that is needed to explain the existence of all contingent things.

This, by the way, is the principle in Science and Philosophy known as "Occam's Razor," after the medieval philosopher William of Occam. The principle directs us always to give precedence to the *simplest*, sufficient explanation, and not to waste our time dreaming up more elaborate possibilities if a simpler one will suffice. People who do not adhere to this principle usually end up these days lost in political conspiracy theories, and elaborate speculations about the activity of UFOs and aliens from outer space on our planet! As we discussed in our previous letters, Krystal, God is the simplest, sufficient explanation for the beginning of the universe, for order and design in the universe, for the Natural Moral Law shining in every human heart, and for the universal human longing for the endless possession of perfect, boundless Good. And here, one God (rather than many) is the simplest, sufficient explanation for the existence of the whole show.

Second, there could not possibly be more than one self-existent being anyway, if a "self-existent being" by definition is Being itself, the power and fullness of all that it can mean "to be." In his book *The Last Superstition*, Edward Feser explains:

> In order for there to be two or more purely actual beings, there would have to be some way of distinguishing them, some feature that one of them had that the others lacked; and

there just couldn't be any such feature. For to lack such a feature is just to have an unrealized potential, and a purely actual being, by definition, has no unrealized potentials…. So again, there is no feature that one purely actual being could have that another could lack, and thus no way even in theory to distinguish one from another. So there couldn't be more than one.[4]

f. If God made everything, then who made God?—what is the "sufficient reason" for *His* existence?

We come back to this question again, from my last letter—and I hope you can see now, Krystal, that this question makes no sense, if we have a clear idea of what the word "God" means for Philosophy. It's like asking "who caused to be the one self-existent being, the one being who does not need to be caused to be?" Clearly, He is the sufficient reason for His own existence—not in the sense that He caused Himself to be (remember my last letter: it is logically impossible for something to cause itself to be, because you have to "be" before you can cause anything at all!), but in the sense that, as self-existent, He did not need to come into being at all. He necessarily always is—or nothing could exist at all! I like the way Catholic author F.J. Sheed puts it:

> Every student of [classical] philosophy has heard the question, and they all know that there *must* be a being which did not need to be made. If nothing existed except *receivers* of existence [i.e., contingent beings] where would existence come from? In order that anything may exist, there must be a being that simply has it. God can confer existence on other beings precisely because he has it in his own right. It is his nature to exist. God does not have to receive existence because he is [the power and fullness of] existence.

Now we understand the name God gave himself. The story is in the third chapter of Exodus. God appeared to Moses in the burning bush. When Moses asked him his name, God said, "I am who am. Thus shalt thou say to the children of Israel: He who is hath sent me to you." This is God's name for himself, I AM. Our name for him is HE IS…. That is the primary truth about God. He is, he exists, with all that existence in its fullness can mean.[5]

Love Always,

Uncle Robert

11. Reasonable Hope

Hi Krystal,

Well, to say the least, you are always full of surprises. I was stunned when I read that you have decided to leave your university, and transfer to a small, ecumenical Christian college in New Brunswick to finish your degree. "Not" you hasten to add, "because I have become some kind of convert to Christianity, but because I have become fed up with the narrowness of the place where I am stuck now, where consideration of the possible God-dimension of things is never taken seriously." Your logic for making this move seems to me to be impeccable:

> To be sane is to be in touch with reality, as much as possible. To be well-educated is to be taught to understand reality, as much as possible. But if there is a God, then He is the *ultimate reality*, the reality behind all other realities. So to go through a college education where the God-dimension of the subjects we study is almost always completely ignored, or completely dissed, is… well… insane.

I'll add an analogy to your logic here. It seems to me that the kind of education you were getting at that secular university was like doing a Physics major, and taking courses on the origins of the universe, and never mentioning the Big Bang. Yet the Big Bang is arguably the initial reality behind all physical realities in this universe. To ignore it—much less deny it without careful consideration—as the beginning of all physical realities in this world, would be… well… insane.

All this is to say that, from what I can see, you have made a good decision. I didn't mean to try to instigate such a change when we started our e-mail dialogue last fall, but I can heartily endorse it now—especially because I know the place you are going quite well, having given lectures there several times in the past. It's a small, friendly place, where the God-side of things is indeed given a fair-hearing, but will certainly not be imposed on you. You will be in good hands.

At the same time, you shared with me your struggles—which have evidently been going on for months now—with the powerful message of a novel you read in French class by Albert Camus: *The Plague*. Now I see more clearly why you said that our dialogue, helpful as it has been to you so far, has not really addressed the "core doubts" that you struggle with. Despite all the evidence and arguments I have marshaled for the existence of God, and for the reality and immortality of the human spirit, the protest against God put forward in that book seems unanswerable to you at the moment. Nobody can put it better than you did in your last letter:

> If there really is a God—the Sufficient Reason for everything that exists, as you said—then how can He permit so much innocent suffering to go on in His world? I mean how could He sit back and watch millions of people—helpless peasants mostly—get wiped out by the bubonic plague that killed 1/3 of the population of Europe in the 14th century, and do nothing about it? How come He permitted Auschwitz and Dachau and Hiroshima and Nagasaki? Why does He let little children die of leukemia, young mothers die of cancer, leave millions of families to die of starvation in Africa, do nothing as He sees wives beaten, unborn children killed in their mother's wombs, husbands and fathers slaughtered in senseless wars, whole towns swept off the map by earthquakes, tornadoes, volcanoes and tsunamis? In short, if there really is a God *why is all this is happening on His watch?*

I hope you won't be shocked by what I have to say this time, Krystal, but the truth is: *Philosophy cannot give us a complete answer to your question.* Human reason can only go so far.

But we also need to set what Philosophy *cannot* tell us against all that it can. If what you wrote, Krystal, is all that we can know about human misery and innocent suffering in the world, then that would indeed be a decisive objection against either the existence or goodness of God; your doubts would be fully justified.

Happily, it isn't all that we can know. Philosophical reason can shed at least some light on the mystery of human suffering.

First of all, Philosophy can show us, beyond a reasonable doubt, that there is an all-powerful, all-seeing, infinitely Good Creator. All that you wrote about suffering, Krystal, does not show that there is anything logically amiss with any of the "pro-God" arguments we discussed in our previous letters. In other words, to be rationally consistent we do not need to reject the existence of God in the face of all the innocent suffering in the world. To begin with, we just need to admit the limitation of our human perspective on these things. We can honestly say "I don't understand why God permits some of the things He does; I definitely don't have the complete answer to these things. But His Knowledge and Wisdom are infinite whereas mine are only finite. If He exists—as Philosophy can show—then He must know the complete answer. A God of infinite knowledge and benevolence could only permit innocent suffering to happen for the sake of at least the possible attainment of some *greater good*, which we cannot fully see—or at least, not yet." To adopt this view, Krystal, allows you to do justice both to the strong arguments in favor of the existence of God, and at the same time to the awful reality of innocent suffering in His world.

Again, from our limited vantage point we may not be able fully to see what that "greater good" could be, but that does not mean it does not exist, or that Philosophy cannot provide us at least with some insights into what God may be up to here.

For example, there is what is called in Philosophy *"The Free Will Defense."* It simply says this: from what we can see, "the lion's share" of all the miseries of human life are directly caused by, and augmented by, the misuse of God's greatest natural gift to us—our freedom to choose. God did not want to create mere robots, whose behavior was completely pre-programmed by their genes and their environment; He did not want to create mere "puppets on a string"—for robots and puppets cannot think for themselves, cannot create anything new or meaningful, and most of all, cannot love. Authentic love, creativity, and knowledge can only arise in beings who are truly free, who *voluntarily* choose to embrace an idea, to envision a new work of art, to reach out and give themselves away for the sake of others. If this is the kind of creature that God was striving to create when He fashioned human beings—if this was the "greater good" He was trying to attain—then He had no choice but to bestow upon us the gift of free-will. But the freedom to think, love, and create, is also the freedom to lie, hate, and destroy. God took the risk of giving human beings true freedom, because He evidently believed the risk was worth it: the "greater good" of enabling human beings to attain true wisdom, creativity, and love was worth it. Do we have the kind of vantage point on the whole story of humanity to tell Him that He was wrong?

"Yes we do!" someone might say. "For it's not that free-will gets misused just by some people and not others. *Everyone* seems to misuse it, to one degree or another. As a result, 'man's inhumanity to man,' wounds every human life, and many of the pages of human history are written in blood. If there really is a God, then He clearly made a serious 'design-flaw' in human nature itself; He is not the 'perfect boundless Good' that your Philosophy claims him to be."

Here again, however, Philosophy has more to say. For the deepest miseries that we inflict on each other come from the misuse of another of the highest gifts that God gave to us: our *interdependence*. Freedom and interdependence go together to make up the twin foundation of the highest human goods. I put it this way in a book manuscript I am writing, Krystal:

> It is only because human lives are free and interdependent that we can experience such blessings as the procreation and nurture of children, familial love and affection, the enrichment of our lives through the development of culture and civilization, and social and cooperative enterprises of all kinds: those that sustain human life with proper food, clothing, shelter, medical care, and creative work opportunities. Human freedom and interdependence make possible love, language, literature, scientific advance, the development of computers and the construction of great cathedrals. At its highest and best, human freedom and interdependence are taken up by divine grace into the experience of loving "communion" in the Body of Christ. However, the same freedom and interdependence which makes all of these goods possible also makes us deeply vulnerable to its misuse, resulting in abuses of human dignity, and injustices of all kinds. In short, we can affect each other's lives so deeply for ill only because we can also affect each other so deeply for good.

So, again, we are faced with the same question: are we in a position to be able to say that God made a big mistake here, and that everything that He made possible for us by giving us true freedom and interdependence is not worth the cost in human suffering? I don't think we are. And unless we are sure that we are, then the innocent suffering in the world, insofar as it results from human vice, and agonizing as it is, does not amount to a strong objection against the existence or goodness of God.

At times, we do seem to live in an "unfair" world, where all too often people suffer from the evil deeds of others, and not just from their own. Does this make God unjust?

There is a deep mystery here, Krystal, I think. My favorite passage from any book on this subject comes from Jerry

Sittser's *A Grace Disguised.* Sittser lost his wife, his mother, and his baby daughter in a fatal car accident, and that led him to ask God the obvious question—and then to hear an interesting answer:

> Why me? Most of us want life not only to be under our control but also to be fair. So when we suffer loss, we claim our right to justice and resent circumstances that get in the way. We demand to live in a society in which virtue is rewarded and vice punished, hard work succeeds and laziness fails, decency wins and meanness loses. We feel violated when life does not turn out that way, when we get what we do not deserve and do not get what we feel we deserve….
>
> Yet over time I began to be bothered by this assumption that I had a right to complete fairness. Granted that I did not deserve to lose three members of my family. But then again, I am not sure I deserved to have them in the first place. Lynda was a woman of superior qualities, and she loved me through some very hard times. My mother lived well and served people to her life's end, and she showed rare sensitivity to me during my rebellious teenage years. Diane Jane sparkled with enthusiasm for life and helped fill our home with noise and excitement. Perhaps I did not deserve their deaths; but I did not deserve their presence in my life either. On the face of it, living in a perfectly fair world appeals to me. But deeper reflection makes me wonder. In such a world I might never experience tragedy; but neither would I experience grace, especially the grace God gave me in the form of three wonderful people whom I lost.[1]

Let's go even deeper, Krystal, because I think Philosophy can shed more light for us on this mystery of innocent suffering.

For instance, reason can tell us that if an infinitely wise and good God gave to humanity many rich blessings as our Creator, blessings such as freedom and interdependence, then

He must have given them to us for a good purpose. Evidently, the talents and gifts He gave to each one of us are to be freely used *precisely to help overcome and relieve the miseries of others*. In other words, God knew that as the result of the highest gifts He gave to us, He would also have to permit the misuse of His gifts, and some evil and suffering in His world, and so He included in His creative design for human life a built-in "immune system," so to speak, to counter-act these miseries.

How do we know this?

Well, first of all, because He gave us some "white-blood cells": not just the physical ones in our bodies, but also the guiding light of the Natural Moral Law. This inner Light that He instilled in every human heart includes a general principle of "benevolence," directed especially toward those who are closest to us, whose needs are most evident to us, and whose needs we can most effectively address: our family members, relatives, friends, and near neighbors. In short, the Natural Law constantly beckons us to reach out and help one another.

In addition, God has given us "vital signs" indicators, to help keep us on the right path. Clearly, if God is pure Spirit, and He has bestowed on every human being a spirit that is a created reflection of His own, then it stands to reason that our spirits were made to do what God's Spirit does: bestow gifts and blessings on others. It is the constant testimony of those who follow the Natural Moral Law, and who reflect God's generous and compassionate Spirit in their own lives, that they experience tremendous inner peace and satisfaction from doing so—a clear sign that this is precisely the way we were meant to live, to fulfill the good purpose for which we were made. The person that lives this way walks with an easily contented spirit, a peaceful conscience, and a quiet heart. The "vital signs," so to speak, are all positive.

Third, it is clear from the reflections of great Philosophers (e.g., Aristotle and Aquinas), that the more we practice virtues such as generosity of spirit and compassion, the stronger those virtues become in us—especially if they are forged and refined in the midst of adversity. This suggests that one of the reasons God permits evils and sufferings in His world is that by facing and overcoming them with virtue, we can grow stronger in spirit. Many philosophical theists, therefore, speak of God's world as *"a vale of soul-making."* To some extent at least, God permits life to be a struggle and a challenge for us for our own good. In other words, life is meant to be more like a physiotherapy center than a rest home!

Fourth, there must be divine medicine for us near at hand. For it is reasonable to assume that a God who asks us to face and overcome suffering and misery in our lives, and in the lives of others, will not leave us to do so on our own. He will come to our aid. At the very least, He will provide us with the spiritual medicine we need for the journey: light and inspiration to guide our steps, strength to enable us to persevere, and pardon and forgiveness when we stumble and fall. That He does so is the constant testimony of those who believe in God down through history (Jews, Christians, philosophical theists and deists of all kinds). Turning to Him in prayer for light and strength, therefore, is not a solely "religious" thing to do—it is a reasonable thing to do for anyone who walks the path of Philosophy.

Finally, can we imagine that if there really is an all-powerful, all-seeing, infinitely benevolent God that He would create such amazing creatures as us, and set before us such difficult challenges, and then let our lives be cut off in the end without hope? Surely, reason alone compels us to believe otherwise. Remember, philosophy, backed up by evidence from science, can show that He gave to each one of us an *immortal spirit*, which means that our destiny must extend beyond the struggles of this world. In other words, if God intended this world to be a "vale of soul-making," then this implies that the immortal souls He gave to us are being fashioned for an immortal purpose. The book of Wisdom in the Bible, chapter 3, drawing upon the ancient Greek heritage of Philosophy, sums it up like this:

But the souls of the righteous are in the hand of God, and no torment will ever touch them. In the eyes of the foolish they seem to have died, and their departure was thought to be an affliction, and their going from us their destruction; but they are at peace. For though in the sight of men they were punished, their hope is full of immortality.

Krystal, I know your "core doubts" (as you put them) do not come solely from philosophical reflection, or from reading that novel by Camus. None of us are "disembodied brains," so to speak—when we think philosophical thoughts, we can only do so in the midst of the circumstances and struggles of our daily lives. And I know that there is not day that goes by that you do not miss your beloved grandmother, who loved you so much, and who was taken from you and your Mom in such a cruel way, through an extended period of physical deterioration and suffering. I am not denying the basis of your grief—I am just asking you to search your heart, and ask yourself: *"Was the suffering and dying of my grandma really the full truth about the end of her story?"* After all, she was a woman who deeply believed in God. She lived a life full of generosity and compassion for others, and constant prayer, and she struggled heroically in her final months to keep her belief and her prayer for others strong to the end. When she died, her hope was "full of immortality," as the book of Wisdom says, and she looked forward to the day when she would be with us all again, in the nearer presence of God, where there is neither sorrow, nor crying nor pain any longer. Would you say now that the beliefs on which she lived and died were tragically mistaken? Was her whole life and her final hope founded on sheer folly? Rather, doesn't Philosophy indicate, in numerous ways, *that your grandma was absolutely right?*

Benjamin Franklin once summed up what decades of philosophical reflection led him to believe about God and about human life in these words:

Here is my Creed: I believe in one God, Creator of the Universe. That he governs it by Providence. That he ought to be worshipped. That the most acceptable Service we render to him is doing good to his other Children. That the soul of Man is immortal, and will be treated with Justice in another Life respecting its conduct in this. These I take to be the fundamental Principles of all sound Religion...[2]

To my mind, Franklin was entirely right. I know that this Philosophy does not answer every agonizing question that plagues us: for example, "Why did God permit this terrible suffering in this particular circumstance? Why doesn't He do more to stop it?" The ancient philosopher Boethius wrote his greatest work after he had been condemned to death for a crime he did not commit. The result was his masterpiece, *The Consolation of Philosophy*. You see, Krystal, he didn't claim that Philosophy alone could supply us with *all* the answers we seek. But it can supply us with some answers: with enough for "consolation" in the midst of affliction, some light for the way, and a reasonable hope for our journeys' end.

Perhaps you will think to yourself: "But that's not enough; it's just not enough to answer all the questions that need answering—and the answers it gives are not enough fully to rescue the human race from evil and guilt, from suffering and death." Well, if that's your perspective, Krystal, I think you are right: Philosophy alone really isn't enough. But it's a great start—big step in the right direction!

And maybe God has other ways of speaking to us than just through Philosophy. I mean why do we think that God is limited to revealing His nature, His character, and His purposes for human life *solely* through what we can demonstrate by our reason alone, reflecting on His creation? Maybe He has a lot more to say to us than Philosophy can contain? Maybe some of the most important things He has to tell us—even about suffering and evil in His world, and His response to them—could only be expressed to us in another way, in fact, in the form of a Cross?

But that, of course, is another story.

Meanwhile, don't lose heart. Gerard Manley Hopkins summed up in a single poem, Krystal, just about everything that I've tried to share with you over the past year, and the ground of all our hope. He expressed it far better than I could ever do:

The world is charged with the grandeur of God.
It will flame out, like shining from shook foil;
It gathers to a greatness, like the ooze of oil
Crushed. Why do men then now not reck his rod?
Generations have trod, have trod, have trod;
And all is seared with trade; bleared, smeared with toil;
And wears man's smudge and shares man's smell: the soil
Is bare now, nor can foot feel, being shod.

And for all this, nature is never spent;
There lives the dearest freshness deep down things;
And though the last lights off the black West went
Oh, morning, at the brown brink eastward, springs —
Because the Holy Ghost over the bent
World broods with warm breast and with ah! bright wings.

Love always,

Uncle Robert

Postscript:
Fragment of a Letter
(On Postmodernism)

With regard to your question, Krystal: I am not surprised that you are finding it hard to "wrap your head around" what your profs really mean by "Postmodernism." It is a diverse and ever-changing cultural and intellectual movement, and therefore rather hard to define. The broadest definition seems to be that Postmodernism (PM for short) is a wholesale attack on the unwarranted optimism of the "modern" era, also known as the "Enlightenment" (that is, roughly the era from the philosopher Rene Descartes around 1650 until the collapse of Communism in the 1980s). What postmodernists find especially objectionable is the boundless confidence that the Enlightenment placed in human reason and science to discover all the truth we need to know about the world in which we live, and to solve all social ills.

Stated that way, I suppose, most Christians would be postmodernists as well! But Postmodernism takes this critique of the Enlightenment much farther than Christianity dares to do. It's a classic case of "the peril of the pendulum" in cultural history, manifest in a radical swing from sole confidence in reason (in the Enlightenment) to *no confidence in reason at all* (in Postmodernism)! For PM rejects all claims of religions and philosophies to possess the objective truth about the world, especially claims to possess an over-arching "worldview" or "meta-narrative" (the "big story") that is allegedly true for all. All comprehensive worldviews are seen as mere "social constructs": intellectually unjustifiable "language games" that mask a desire for power over others through imposing on them one's vision of "the truth"—as well as a desire simply to cope with the anxieties of life and death. In other words, religious and philosophical "meta-narratives" are not really the product of human reason: rather, they are the product of fear, anxiety, and the will to power. As a result, the wise person will seek for tolerance for all points of view, for no one has any more objective claim to possessing universal truth than anyone else.

We have already met some aspects of Postmodernism in our previous correspondence, Krystal. Remember our brief discussion of how "religion" is often accused of fostering violence and oppression [Letter #3], and our brief look at the thought of the 19th century philosopher Friedrich Nietzsche [Letter #8]—he is considered a great forerunner of the PM movement.

Anyway, here are a few questions you can ask your PM professors and friends, just to "get the ball rolling" of a proper, critical assessment of all this.

1) Isn't PM itself a kind of worldview or meta-narrative (after all, it purports to tell us what *really* lies behind human culture and the quest for truth)—and so, isn't PM on its own terms just another "language game," with no more solid, objective reasons to back it up than anything else? If so, why should we take it seriously? As James Sire puts it: "If we hold that all linguistic utterances are power plays, then that utterance itself is a power play, and no more likely to be proper than any other."[1] Sound familiar? We're back to the problem of Self-referential Absurdity again, Krystal. PM, in its pure forms at least, just saws off the branch it is sitting on!

2) The Postmodernist rightly objects to the way Pre-modern religions and Modern political ideologies often became oppressive. By claiming to know the truth *for* all they sometimes sought to impose their vision of truth *on* all— from the Crusades and the Inquisition to the French Revolution's Reign of Terror and the Communist labor camps. The assault of radical Islam on human rights today is just the latest incarnation of this cultural sickness.

The trouble is that by undermining the rational foundations and objective truth of *all* philosophical and religious ideas, PM has also undermined the objective foundations of all moral codes—and thereby undermined any basis for objecting to social injustice and oppression in the first place! After all, why should we stand up for human rights and freedom for all people? Presumably because social tyranny is oppressive: it uses lies and propaganda to impose its ideology on all, and imprisons and murders those who disagree. But if we cannot ever really know the objective truth about human life and the world in which we live, how can we possibly tell the difference between a "lie" and "the truth"? And what is wrong with tyranny, murder, and oppression anyway if they happen to get me and my allies what we want, since, according to PM, we have no access (through either human reason or divine revelation) to any universal moral code of respect for life and liberty that we all ought to follow?

Guess what: Self-referential Absurdity again! PM, in its pure forms, at least, undermines its own moral critique of social oppression!

3) In its eagerness to demolish Enlightenment rationalism, doesn't the PM movement also overlook those aspects of contemporary research that actually tend to *support* the Modernist claim that there are truths about human life and the world that are available to all and apply to all? For example, Krystal, look up Todorov and Chomsky's research on the cross-cultural phenomena of common grammatical structures in human language. The point is that human beings structure and express their thoughts in fairly similar ways in every culture in the world (which, of course, is what makes it possible for us to learn foreign

131

languages and communicate with people of other cultures). Or how about the field of Developmental Psychology, where cross-cultural stages of human cognitive and moral growth were discovered by researchers such as Piaget and Kolberg? And how about CS Lewis' famous book *The Abolition of Man*, where he presented evidence of certain core moral values that are common to every human civilization down through history? It's also pretty hard to dismiss mathematics as just another culturally relative, socially constructed "language game"—and mathematics, of course, is one of the foundational tools of the natural sciences.

These are just a few examples. The PM movement has surely "overshot the mark" in its wholesale critique of the capacity of human reason to discover the truth about what it is to be a human being, and about the world around us. Such radical skepticism is simply unjustified. And if you don't believe me, listen to this humorous illustration of the point by the novelist Robert Capon:

> The skeptic is never for real. There he stands, cocktail in hand, left arm draped languorously on one end of the mantelpiece, telling you that he can't be sure of anything, not even of his own existence. I'll give you my secret method of demolishing universal skepticism in four words. Whisper to him: "Your fly is open." If he thinks knowledge is so all-fired impossible, why does he always look?[2]

Don't worry about the present ascendancy of PM on your campus, Krystal. It won't last. For now it is intellectual "flavor of the month," but I am pretty sure it will fizzle-out soon enough. The trouble with PM is that the human mind naturally seeks the truth; we want to know why the "whole show" is here, and what human life is meant for. PM tells us that we cannot answer such questions with any confidence at all. It leaves us wallowing in *skepticism* (we can't know the truth), *nihilism* (there is no truth to know anyway), and *moral relativism* (there is no objective right or wrong): it's a "starvation diet" for the human spirit. Most people cannot live on that thin gruel for very long. So here's a prediction: look for the New Age Movement, and for Christianity, to pick up more and more refugees from PM despair in the decades to come.

I think PM is doomed for another reason as well: postmodernists have hardly any kids. Through contraception and abortion, PM couples usually have as few children as possible, just because they have hardly any motivation to make the kinds of sacrifices necessary to build families. After all, from a PM perspective: what's the point? Life has no discernible meaning or purpose—anyway, nothing that is not swallowed up by death in the end. Most PM couples, therefore, just focus their energies on living as comfortably as possible before the darkness closes in on them: a kind of *anesthetized narcissism*. Family life, on the other hand, involves loving sacrifice for others founded on hope for the future. No hope equals no family. Postmodernists are simply euthanizing themselves....

Chapter 2: The Problem with "Nothing Buttery"

1. Pierre Simon Laplace, *A Philosophical Essay on Probability*, as cited in Wikipedia.org/wiki/Laplace's_demon .

2. Rodney D. Holder, *Nothing But Atoms and Molecules: Probing the Limits of Science*. Cambridge: The faraday Institute, 2008, p. 44.

3. Ibid., p. 89.

4. Ibid., pp. 85-86.

5. Ibid., p. 32.

Chapter 3: The Human Spirit

1. Pope St. John Paul II, encyclical *Centesimus Annus* (1991), iv. 44.

2. F.J. Sheed, *Theology for Beginners*. Ann Arbor: Servant Books, 1981, p. 14.

Chapter 4. The Difference it Makes

1. Dinesh D'Souza, *Life After Death: The Evidence*. Washington, DC: Regnery Publishing, 2009, pp. 39-40.

2. Ibid., p. 198.

3. Ibid., pp. 60-61.

4. Holder, *Nothing But Atoms and Molecules,* pp. 10-11.

5. William Lane Craig, *Reasonable Faith*. Wheaton: Crossway, third edition, 2008, p. 73.

Chapter 5: The Secret of the Human Heart

1. C.S. Lewis, *The Weight of Glory and Other Essays*. San Francisco: Harper Collins, 2001 edition, pp. 42-43 and 31.

2. C.S. Lewis, *The Joyful Christian*. New York: Macmillan, 1977, pp. 28-30

3. C.S. Lewis, *The Pilgrim's Regress*. Grand Rapids: Eerdmans, 1992 edition, PP. 202-203.

4. Bertrand Russell, *The Autobiography of Bertrand Russell*. Boston: Little, Brown and Co., 1968, pp. 95-96.

5. C.S. Lewis, *Mere Christianity*. New York: Macmillan, 1961 edition, pp. 104-105.

6. C.S. Lewis, *The Problem of Pain*. San Francisco: Harper Collins, 2001 edition, pp. 149-151.

Chapter 6: A Message in the Stars

1. Holder, *Nothing But Atoms* and Molecules, p. 153.

2. Peter Kreeft, *Fundamentals of the Faith*. San Francisco: Ignatius Press, 1988, pp. 26027.

3. A.C. Grayling, *The God Argument*. London: Bloomsbury, 2013, p. 81.

4. Ibid., p.80.

5. D'Souza, *Life After Death*, p. 85.

6. Cited in Anthony Flew, *There is a God*. New York: Harper Collins, 2008 edition, p.

7. Ibid., pp. 105-106.

8. Cited in D'Souza, *Life After Death*, p. 98.

9. Ibid., p. 99.

Chapter 7: The Inner Light

1. Lewis, *Mere Christianity*, p. 4.

2. Ibid., pp. 5-6

3. Ibid., p. 24.

4. Cited in peterkreeft.com/topics-more/20_arguments-gods-existence. htm#14.

5. Ibid.

6. J.H. Newman, *A Grammar of Assent*. C.F. Harold, ed. London: Longmans, 1947 edition, p.83.

Chapter 8: The New Age, and Other Options

1. Lewis, *Mere Christianity*, pp. 30-31.

2. James Sire, *The Universe Next Door: A Basic Worldview Catalog*. Downer's Grove: Inter-Varsity Press, third edition, 1997, pp. 70-71.

3. *Ibid.*, p. 66.

4. Cited in Morton Kelsey, *Healing and Christianity*. Minneapolis: Augsburg, 1995, p. 242.

Chapter 9: Physics and the Self-Creating Universe

1. Stephen Hawking, *The Grand Design.* New York: Bantam Books, 2010, p. 180.

2. Stephen M. Barr, "Much Ado About Nothing: Stephen Hawking and the Self-Creating Universe," from First Things, September, 2010, at firstthings.com/web-exclusives/2010/09/much-ado-about-Idquonothingrdquo-stephen-hawking-and-the-self-creating-universe.

3. *Ibid.*

4. D'Souza, *Life After Death*, p. 83.

5. The full article can be found at michaelhorner.com.

6. Craig, *Reasonable Faith*, p.114-115.

7. Boethius, *The Consolation of Philosophy.* London: Penguin Edition, 1999, book III, p.67.

Chapter 10: The Wonder of Existence

1. T.Z. Lavine, *From Socrates to Sartre: The Philosophic Quest.* New York: Bantam Books, 1984, p.168.

2. George F. Thomas, *Religious Philosophies of the West.* New York: Scribner's, 1965, p. 232.

3. Ibid., p. 197.

4. Edward Feser, *The Last Superstition.* South Bend: St. Augustine Press, 2008, pp. 97-98.

5. Sheed, *Theology for Beginners*, p. 18.

Chapter 11: Reasonable Hope

1. Jerry Sittser, *A Grace Disguised*. Grand Rapids: Zondervan, second edition, 2004, pp. 124, and 126.

2. Cited in David L. Homes, *Faiths of the Founding Fathers*. New York: Oxford University Press, 2006, pp. 56-57.

Chapter 12: Postscript on Modernism

1. Sire, *The Universe Next Door*, p. 187.

2. Cited in Sire, *The Universe Next Door*, p. 86 .

Made in the USA
Middletown, DE
02 December 2015